HOW TO RESTORE
Upholstery

OSPREY
RESTORATION
GUIDE 7

HOW TO RESTORE

Upholstery

Tony Fairweather

Published in 1985 by Osprey Publishing Limited,
12–14 Long Acre, London WC2E 9LP
Member company of the George Philip Group

Sole distributors for the USA

Osceola, Wisconsin 54020, USA

British Library Cataloguing in Publication Data

Fairweather, Tony
    How to restore Car Upholstery.—(Osprey restoration guide; 7)
    1. Automobile——Upholstery
    I. Title
    629.2′6   TL255

ISBN 0-85045-623-1

Editor Tim Parker

Filmset and printed by
BAS Printers Limited, Over Wallop, Hampshire

CONTENTS

Introduction

This book is divided into six chapters, each with the intention of giving the enthusiast a good basic insight into the restoration, and indeed in most instances the manufacture of the various facets that go to make up the complete car interior.

I have tried, wherever possible, to assume that you, the individual reading this book, are doing so because you have a desire to 'have a go' and will eventually be able to complete perhaps more of the restoration of the total car than would have been possible prior to the purchase of *How To Restore Upholstery*.

Each area or facet of the car interior is dealt with to assist, particularly if you are a novice, with the possibility of achieving really satisfying and worthwhile results, but these results need care and concentration as well as enthusiasm!

It is with this thought in mind that it is necessary to adopt the practice or practising of trimming work on spare or scrap material first, whether this be marking out, cutting, machining, assembling etc. . . .

Car interiors cannot be rushed or hurried, they can be likened to the experience of a good lady, give her the chance and the time and generally this will yield satisfying and pleasing results.

Examples of the interiors of vehicles from Europe and the USA are featured, as well as many from Great Britain, so there should be ample scope for comparison.

Finally, there are two very useful chapters dealing with tools and fabrics, and hints on sewing machine usage, enough basic information and tips to make a confident start.

The have a go dilemma!
Don't despair 'cause most of it's there,
old springs and hooks even horses' hair!
For even though its rotten within,
photographs and sketching will fill you in.
But should you pull it all apart
without considering the trimmer's art,
beware of what lies for you in store
for without this knowledge you cannot adore

To the grave, or to be resurrected? Difficult for even the professional, let alone the keen enthusiast. Therefore, leave it to the professional and whether it be a Rolls-Royce or Mini, seek advice first before disturbing anything!
Most professional upholsterers/trimmers, will give an estimate free of charge. However, if you do incur expenses, make sure that you do gain his advice and not just a nicely typed estimate!

the finished product all smart and trim
for being too hasty can be a sin.

Seriously speaking, to the grave or to be resurrected? Difficult for even the professional, let alone the keen enthusiast. Therefore, leave it to the professional and whether it be a Rolls-Royce or a Morris Mini, seek advice first before disturbing anything.

Most professional restorers/trimmers will give advice and an estimate free of charge, but even if they do want payment, this is often well worth the expense. However, if you do have to incur expenses, make sure that you do gain real advice and not just a nicely typed estimate.

My special thanks to Maurice for his invaluable assistance with the practicalities of trimming.

To Paul Amos, Mike Key, Geoff Palmer, John Burns, and my wife Rita, for their help with photographic assignments. To my family for being so considerate during the many hours with my head buried, and to Lionel Burrell for giving me the opportunity to put pen to paper, without which this book would not have been possible.

Tony Fairweather

Chapter 1 | Tools, materials, preparation

1   General tools

Many of the tools employed in the refurbishing of car interiors are to be found in the average tool shed and/or garage.

I have classified these under this heading of general hand tools and include the following list as a guide:

Hammer—general purpose, cross pein, ball pein or similar

Shears or large scissors

Sharp knife or Stanley-type knife—plus an emery board

G cramps or similar

Mole grips or wrench

Tape measure—imperial and metric segments

Screwdrivers—plain, Phillips—and Posidrive (depending on car)

Pincers

Pliers

Suitable spanners and socket sets

Tack lifter or awl

2   Special tools

Staple lifter*

An invaluable tool where staples have been used in the assembly of any part of car trim and upholstery.

One of the most common places to find staples is in the fixing of fabrics to trim boards, i.e., trim boards as found on the inside of doors, etc.

When staples have been employed, it is difficult to use pliers or pincers as there is little to get hold of and hence the staple lifter with its very slim end is pushed under the centre of the staple, levered downwards and in turn draws the staple out.

If, however, a pair of pliers has to be used, it is wise to lever up the staple with a slim screwdriver, but take care not to slip and stab the other hand supporting the workpiece.

Hollow punches*

The hollow punch is extremely useful when needing to cut holes in carpets. Such as the holes needed to allow freedom of movement for the clutch, brake and possibly the throttle pedal.

A block of lead or piece of hard wood is used, supported on a sturdy bench. The carpet, leather or fabric is positioned over the lead block with the hole ready marked.

Select the correct diameter of punch, (these may be either metric or Imperial size) locate in position ensuring

Just some of the tools necessary to set about restoring the trimming of your car. From the top, heavy duty staple gun, rather expensive to buy, but can often be hired from various tool hire shops. Underneath is a magnetic headed hammer, a good, slim pair of scissors and a stuffing stick that can be made in under an hour at the cost of a few spare pieces of material

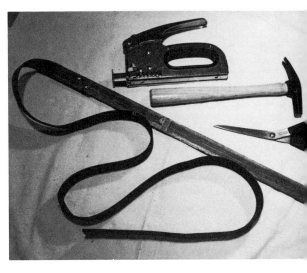

that the punch is at 90 degrees to the surface to be cut and with a ball pein hammer, give the end of the punch a sharp blow.

This then leaves a crisply cut hole that is difficult, if not impossible, to achieve with a knife or scissors.

As for the expense of purchasing one or more hollow punches, you can offset the cost by knowing that they can also be invaluable when it comes to making holes in gasket

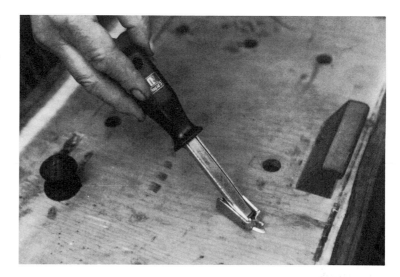

The staple lifting tool. For speed and ease of removal, this inexpensive tool is well worth considering if the vehicle you are going to tackle has plenty of fixings of this type

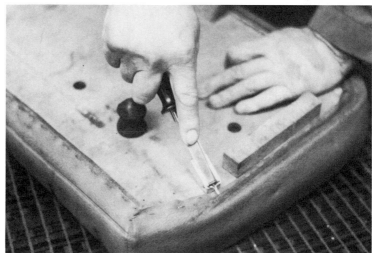

Using the staple lifter to lever out one of the numerous staples from this seat base board takes a matter of minutes. If you have to resort to a screwdriver and pliers you will need a lot of patience and muscle power to cope, especially if a number of staples break. This rarely occurs if using the staple lifter

materials for the mechanical components of your car.

Stuffing sticks, *Staple gun (heavy duty), *Magnetic hammer (details of their use are given in appropriate chapters).

Tools listed under the *General tools* heading are needed for almost every trimming job on the motor car as well as bench work.

Those listed under *Special tools* are only necessary when

Magnetic hammers vary considerably in their capacity to tackle other jobs. This particular one has a claw head for the levering out of tacks by inserting the claw under the head. It is often necessary to start to loosen each tack with an awl or tack lifter first. At the bottom right of the picture is a small disc of steel and this should be replaced on the magnetic head of the hammer after the completion of each task in order to preserve the magnetic field.
The scissors in the picture are shown to give an indication of the size needed compared with the length of the hammer shaft

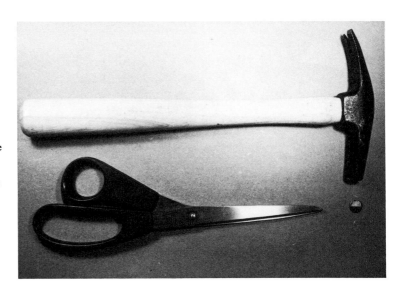

This type of heavy duty stapling machine is adequate for all your trimming needs. A professional trimmer however will often have a pneumatic powered stapler giving rapid insertion of each staple together with the capacity to fire through very thick seams etc.

contemplating specific items of trim manufacture, so read that particular section to identify the tools necessary to accomplish such a task before considering the purchase of the same.

Special tools marked with an * asterisk are not necessary but desirable to make life easier. Without these, the job can still be completed, but requires more ingenuity and effort to achieve the same results!

3 Fabrics

The materials as used in the upholstery of the motor car, for seats, headlinings and doors have been many and varied. Those employed in motor cars of the earlier 'collectable' period have tended to have been superseded by more modern materials, mostly of the 'man-made' variety.

These materials have changed for a number of reasons, partly due to technological advances and partly because manufacturers wanted to 'de-skill' the job of car trimming in order that production rates could increase by employing more semi-skilled labour.

Listed are the main materials that have been employed since 1940, up to the 1970s, organized in order of their introduction to the motor car interior:

Leather, Coach cloth, Rexine, Leathercloth, Vinyl, Vinyl Stockinette (woven backed), Bedford cord, Vianide, Spanish cloth, Brushed nylon and velour.

The identification and matching of the many and varied materials, fabrics etc., that have been used over the years in the trimming of the motor car, can be assisted very often by original sales literature.

These normally specify what was available for a specific model of vehicle and its compatability with the remaining interior and exterior paintwork colour/s.

Other sources of supply that are invaluable regarding this information can be car clubs, manufacturers and various archives up and down the country. The great thing is just to ask someone, if you are unsure, and sooner or later someone else or an organization will be recommended to you that can actually assist.

Of course, once you have found the relevant information, it doesn't mean to say that the material is still available for your vehicle. The hunt is then on to find a supplier who has some old but new stock, i.e., new material that has been in storage for a long time. This part, the searching for materials, for parts etc., I find both interesting and rewarding, for it brings one in touch with so many genuinely helpful people.

Two examples of a full size hide as supplied by Connolly Brothers The hide laid out on the bench with drawers beneath is a second grade and as such has a number of visible unacceptable faults. Therefore, the pieces to be cut from patterns have to be positioned in such a manner as to work around these problems. The other hide shown is a top grade or grade one, the sort of quality expected by Rolls-Royce and Jaguar. Although this hide may have some visible faults, they are so small that with careful cosmetic colouring, they are perfectly acceptable for this standard

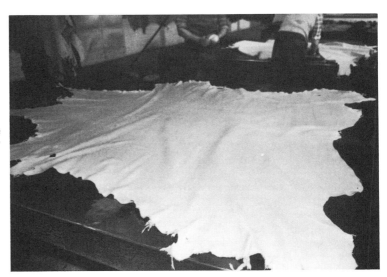

4   Adhesives

Most adhesives as used in the fixing of car interior trim are of the 'contact' type. In other words, each surface to be attached is applied with adhesive. This is allowed to become 'touch dry'. When this stage has been reached, the two surfaces are brought together and the contact between them causes an immediate suction action. Further pressure is then applied to remove any air bubbles etc., but once this point has been reached it is impossible to move without tearing off and carrying out the same process all over again. Hence, it is essential to get the sequence of contact adhesives correct the 'first' time. A good quality adhesive is Dunlop S.1358 in litre cans, or its equivalent.

Two safety hints to remember:

Firstly, always work in an atmosphere that is well ventilated, to ensure the fumes given off are not inhaled.

Secondly, check with the instructions on the container as to its suitability when in use. Failure to do so may cause rapid corrosion of the metal body that the fabric has been attached to or the fabric itself may melt or disintegrate due to the interaction between the adhesive and the fabric. (This often happens if the incorrect glue is used with vinyl fabrics.)

5   Preparation

The essence of achieving good results is to commence in the right manner, in other words, start off with a clear work area and one that is free from sharp edges or protrusions that inevitably cause snags later.

To help guard against the above, as well as keep the work piece clean and non-slip, it pays to tack or glue a scrap of fabric, vinyl or carpet to the top of the work bench. Within reason, the thicker this covering is the better, with carpet or moquette probably being the most suitable, but almost any clean scrap of fabric is better than nothing. Avoid nylon and other slippery surfaces.

Choose a bench area large enough for the job in hand for there is nothing more frustrating than trying to mark-out on a surface far smaller than the fabric being worked on. Most fabrics are supplied in either 48 in. or 54 in. widths, so bear this in mind.

Lighting is also important. Whenever possible work in natural light. When this cannot be arranged, use good, clean, adequate false lighting, or leave the job until either of the previous options are possible. Many a mishap is caused through poor lighting, so don't fall into this trap for the sake of saving a few hours, or even days. You will usually regret the results!

Before actually starting on the job to be tackled, note that you have all the necessary items available. It pays to check little incidental items such as the colour of the thread

Both pictures demonstrate the useful effect of the work bench covered with moquette material. The operation of using the staple lifter and the pneumatic stapling gun both require a good deal of pushing on the workpiece across the bench. The moquette offers a non-stop surface that is comfortable to work on. Having said this, I am only referring to the workbench, not the sewing machine table surface where a smooth work area *is* essential

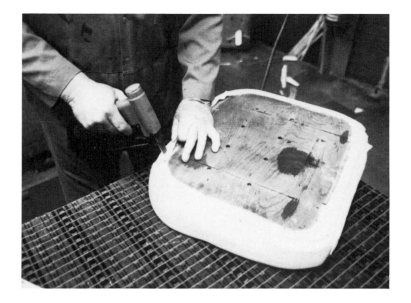

in the machine; will it suit the job you are about to start? Is the machine needle too large, or too small for the fabric to be stitched? You have almost certainly arranged the cover materials and the like, so go forth and make a start. Don't be too ambitious with the first piece of work. Choose something reasonably straightforward, and don't forget, always try any work on the sewing machine on a piece of scrap fabric prior to getting to grips with the actual material to be used for the job in hand. This will ensure that you can check whether (a) the stitch tension is correct for the thickness and number of materials to be machined, and (b) that the number of stitches per inch or per centimetre is adequate. This practice session will also give you a very good idea of the 'feel' for the new fabric. Some fabrics slide over one another more easily than others.

Chapter 2 | Hints on sewing machines and their usage

1   Sewing machines—the various types

The difference between the 'home' machine and the industrial machine is basically one of capacity, in every sense of the word.

Having said this, and in relation to straight stitch machines, there are three approximate areas of work for which each type are designed to cope with:

1 The lightweight 'household' machines. For domestic use only.
2 The 'light industrial' dressmaking sewing machine.
3 The 'heavy industrial' upholstery/car trim sewing machine.

Firstly, each machine has a maximum needle size capacity. For example, the lightweight household machine will generally have a maximum needle size of 100, the light industrial in the region of 135–140, whereas the heavy industrial will have a large needle capacity of 180–190 size. The needle size has the effect of governing the thickness or number of thicknesses to be machined, together with the capacity or thicknesses of thread that is possible to pass through that particular needle.

Secondly, both the light and heavy industrial machines have a comparatively large size motor drive, with a separate clutch, in comparison to the 'home' lightweight which has no clutch and a very small motor. Hence, with the larger motor capacity to draw on, plus the larger needle/thread size, both industrial machines are capable of coping with much heavier work than their lightweight home counterpart.

Having said this, all three types of machine will, with

An example of needles: at the bottom are two for the home or domestic machine, numbering 70 and 100 respectively. Whereas two of the considerably larger needles for the heavy duty industrial machine are shown on the top, numbering 160 and 180

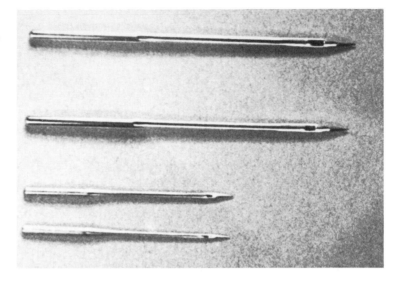

extreme care, cope (albeit on a limited scale) with the 'one off' jobs. But, as one of the members of my restoration class admitted recently, he had 'borrowed' his wife's lightweight machine, only to find that after about 20 minutes' work, he had made the machine unusable. He promptly went out and bought her a new machine, just in time to find her wanting to use the 'useless' burnt out machine that he had overloaded the night before! So, beware!

Thirdly, the bobbin capacity of the heavy industrial machine is far greater than that of either of the smaller machines. This means that the volume of work can be greater prior to the re-threading of the bobbin, hence saving time.

You may be asking yourselves what is the best machine to suit your needs. As for price, a good condition, second-hand, lightweight industrial machine will start from approximately £60–£70 upwards, whereas a good condition heavy industrial machine will commence at £250 upwards, or approximately the price of a new home machine. Usually anything less than this is either an extremely good bargain, or more than likely needs a considerable amount of work carried out prior to making it an effectively 'good condition' machine.

Costs of such machines will of course be considered

more than once if you are contemplating replacing your collector's car interior. But, depending on what type and make of manufacture of machine that you purchase, it is very often a case of 'dead money' until such time as when you want to sell the machine after the 'renovation job' on the car. This usually means a sale of the machine to someone else in a similar position and at a respectably similar price to what you paid for the machine in the not too distant past.

One of the most significant parts to look for on any sewing machine, whatever its capacity, is the size of the drive shaft and number of screws that locate the bobbin case to that shaft. This is important because both of the factors will govern the ease, difficulty or otherwise of the ability for that machine to stay correctly timed.

Many small capacity machines will have a drive shaft rod diameter of only $\frac{1}{4}$ in. with just one screw locating the bobbin case, whereas the industrial machine will have a shaft ranging from probably $\frac{5}{16}$ to $\frac{1}{2}$ in. This, coupled with three locating screws for the bobbin case, means that the chance of the bobbin case slipping on the drive shaft is more unlikely, particularly when stitching thick components such as carpets and the material to bind them with.

Having stated what to look for, the best method of deciding if an individual machine is suitable for your needs is to take some samples of what you wish to stitch with you. Try them on the machine. If it copes *easily*, without breaking the needle, overloading the motor i.e. driving 'flat out' but very slowly or breaking the thread, then if that is the maximum you want to cope with, go ahead and purchase. You should, with this testing and its desired results, be well satisfied.

The following numbers are offered as examples of industrial sewing machines, and as such are a guide. All numbers shown here refer to the Singer Sewing Machine Company's products:

331 K5   With walking foot. Good.
331 K4   Without walking foot. Good
95 K10   Unsuitable.
95 K40   OK.*

Far right **A modern Toyota industrial machine with 'walking foot' capability. If this is what one can afford, then the ease of the workpiece through the machine will be achieved with less effort and inherent skill from the operator. Having said this, the expense involved in purchasing such a machine, even second hand, is not easily justified unless a great deal of trimming work is contemplated**

Right **In this close view of the Singer 31K, the foot is in the raised position showing the sizeable clearance. Incidentally, just to demonstrate the power of this type of machine, I have taken a 160 size needle through $\frac{3}{8}$ in. thick plywood, the only addition required being the need to lubricate the thread**

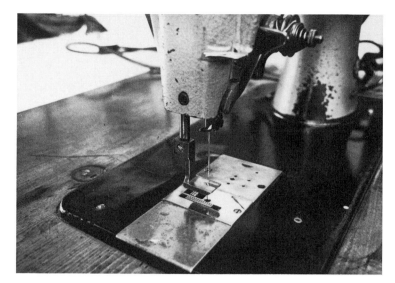

Below **This view is of the 'head' of a Singer 31K heavy industrial sewing machine and is of the fixed foot type**

Diagram I

Sewing machine with 'Fixed Foot'
The arrows show direction of movement
        Left – Clamp foot
        Right – Needle stroke

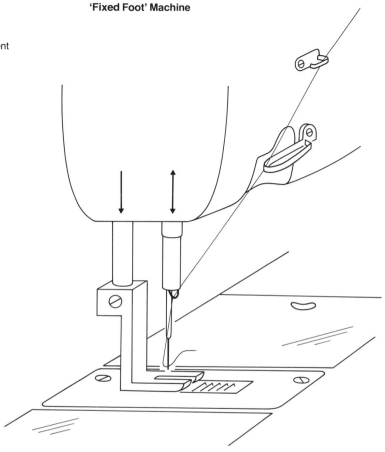

95 K60   OK With reverse.★
95 KVS   Special. OK.★
★Machines marked thus are really for dressmaking, not heavy work, so bear this in mind when considering purchase.

2   'Fixed foot' and 'walking foot' machines

Most of the inexpensive industrial sewing machines have a fixed clamp foot and this is satisfactory for many materials. However, with thick materials and in particular

Diagram 2

Sewing machine with 'Walking Foot'
The arrows show the direction of movement
　　　　Left – Clamp foot
　　Centre – Walking foot
　　　Right – Needle stroke

'Walking Foot' Machine

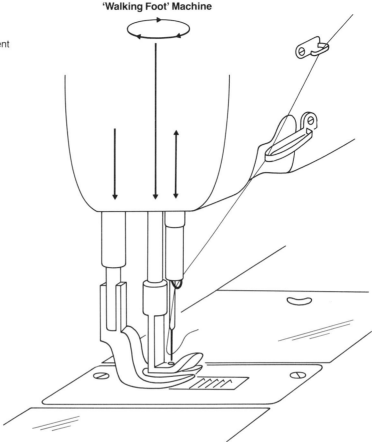

leather, vinyl, plus the stitching of thick components such as piping, the addition of a walking foot machine is invaluable.

This does not mean to say that thick materials, etc. cannot be stitched on a 'fixed' foot machine, but that the feeding of the material through the walking foot is almost automatic, requiring less effort and is thus more easy to control.

With the fixed foot machine, the material requires careful and even assistance through the needle/clamp foot area. Using both hands to hold the work, draw the material towards the back of the machine as the needle punches through the material, whilst simultaneously ensuring that the workpiece is accurately steered.

Walking foot machines require little else other than the steering of the workpiece through the stitching area of the machine, occasionally lifting the foot over extra thick areas to ensure continuity. However, these machines cost con-

Diagram 3

Threading the machine
A typical set up
Look to manufacturer's
instructions for variations

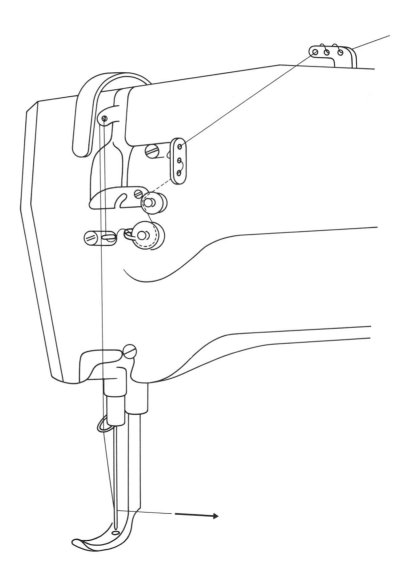

siderably more and careful thought is needed to decide if this is justified.

3 Adjustments for sewing machines

Threading the machine

Before commencing any work on the sewing machine, whether this be to stitch the binding trim onto the edge of carpets, or alternatively to stitch up a 'plastic' headlining, it is most important to ensure that the stitch tension is adjusted to give optimum results.

Bear in mind that the tensioning set up for one type of fabric will not necessarily be adequate for an entirely different fabric. Apart from the thickness of fabrics to be machined, the 'drag' factor when the thread is drawn through the fabrics in question, is equally important. Some materials to be joined, i.e. leather, may require a 'lubricated' thread. This can be achieved by one of two methods. Either, to have the thread pass through an oil bath (as situated on top of most industrial machines), or to immerse the complete spool of thread into an acceptable lubricant prior to fitting onto the machine. (A light oil such as sewing machine oil or household oil will suffice.)

The purpose of the lubricant is to reduce the drag of the thread as it passes through the leather and thus reduce, even eliminate, the risk of either the thread breaking or stitches being missed out completely.

An illustration gives three examples of thread tension. The first has the problem of the thread passing through the needle being too loose, the second too tight and the third sectional view gives the optimum tension created by the correct amount of tension on the machine.

Adjustment of thread tension

Basically there are two areas where the thread may be tensioned on a sewing machine. These consist of adjustment on the machine head and adjustment below the machine head, i.e. the bobbin case, etc. The latter is normally 'pretensioned' by the manufacturer on the spring arm of the bobbin case. Should this give rise to trouble, consult your local sewing machine shop.

If, however, you wish to adjust the needle tension on

Diagram 4

Sewing Machine – Thread Tensions

ose needle thread

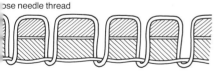

ght needle thread

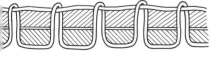

e optimum stitch

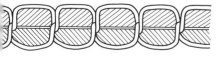

the machine head, this is a quite simple matter. To start with carry out a trial run on a piece of scrap to determine whether the tension is too tight or too loose. Having established this, proceed to check the machine in the following manner:

1 Ensure that the machine is threaded in the correct manner. Many of the problems associated with thread tension are due to incorrect thread-up. Check the route of the thread with the machine manufacturer's handbook. (This route itself gives a degree of tension).
2 Having checked '1', adjust the clamp pressure on the 'clutch'. Slacken if tension is too great, tightening if tension is too loose. Try machine again on test piece. Make further adjustments if necessary.

Stitches per inch
NOTE: The stitches per inch should be adjusted *prior* to

The photograph at the top gives a view of four different clamp feet for the sewing machine, whilst the lower picture depicts the shape of the underside of each foot

On the left in each case is a spring loaded standard clamp foot with a flat base, whilst the remainder are various types of piping clamp feet. The second from right is also spring loaded

The advantage of spring loaded clamp feet is their allowance to accommodate extra thick seams etc., with greater ease, but their assistance to clamp the work really tight is sometimes to be desired. It all depends on the type of material being stitched, thickness and of course the experience of the operator and his or her familiarity with the machine

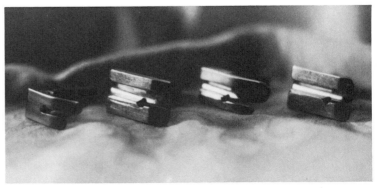

The workpiece pressing under the piping foot clearly demonstrates the piping cord coming in from the bottom left. To the right of the piping foot, the stitched piping is now ready to be attached to the appropriate seat component.
This piping foot is of the 'fixed' non-walking foot type and is not spring loaded at the heel

With piping foot fixed to sewing machine, the piping is stitched to the fluted section. The cuts in the piping flange are there to assist the piping round what is a relatively 'tight' corner

adjusting for thread tension. As a guide, ten stitches per inch is usually satisfactory for most car trimming exercises.

Any more stitches per inch are liable to cut through the material being machined. This is particularly the case when dealing with leather and leathercloth.

4   Use of piping feet

Types of foot

These vary in depth and width to accommodate a variety of piping sizes and material thicknesses. The important feature is to ensure that the stitch line is immediately adjacent to the piping in order to grip the piping cord in a snug and well fitting manner.

Sketches of the profiles of each clamp foot are shown as viewed from the front of the machine, i.e. as sitting where the machinist would operate from. These are compared with a standard clamping foot. Many varieties of piping foot attachments can be purchased to screw onto the bed of the machine, but the cost of these makes them suitable only for volume production work.

Method of use

Raise the standard clamp foot, with the needle at the top of the stroke. Take a screwdriver, unscrew the clamp screw for the foot until sufficiently slack to be able to remove the existing foot. Place in position the selected piping foot, making sure the needle will locate through the foot in an unobstructed manner. Tighten the clamp screw, ready for work.

Having cut material to size and piping to length, fold the material in half at one end over the piping cord. Locate both under the piping foot, ensuring the cord is positioned on the left and the needle ready for stitching on the right. Bring down the piping foot to the workpiece and commence stitching, stopping periodically to fold the next section of material over the piping cord before continuing further.

The same technique is employed when joining the piped section to, for example, a seat cover and border; the only difference being that all three pieces are fed through the piping foot at the same time, covering fabrics face to face.

Chapter 3 | Headlinings—How to make and fit

Here is one of the jobs that most people can tackle, not just the removing and fitting, but the manufacture of a new headlining on a 'home' sewing machine. Most hand, treadle or electric machines used by housewives will cope with the materials needed for headlinings.

1   Materials

The brushed cloth used in car headlinings from the 1940s and early 1950s was very much the same in appearance although varied considerably in quality. Cars of the later monocoque/integral body era (those without a separate chassis) moved away from the brushed cotton or nylon headlinings to plastic or vinyl materials. Only the more expensive or coach–built limousine cars have tended to keep fitting the brushed coach cloth!

The reasons for moving from the coach cloth to the modern 'plastics' were numerous, but primarily the latter were easier to fit and stretch into position, lighter in weight and appearance, and much cheaper to produce. Coach cloth, on the other hand, is generally more 'comfortable' for the car's occupants. It produces a warmer and quieter vehicle, thus enhancing the driving experience.

2   Method of fitment

Almost without exception, all headlinings in the 'collectable' period were suspended on what is known as 'list' wires or bars. These were either wooden battens as on cars in the earlier part of this period or metal rods.

Whichever the case on your vehicle, it is important to note that the length of each bar is very often individual, the widest fitted in the centre of the car, whilst the shorter ones tending to be at the front and rear.

List wires or bars are passed through a stitched loop on the upper part of the headlining *after* machining has been completed.

As for fixing the sides of the lining, this may vary considerably. Ranging from tacks fixed into either a wooden batten or compressed board, to a crimped flange (as on the Ford Anglia), or as in many cases on 1960s vehicles, glued in position and then finished off with the clamping action of the door draught or screen seal rubber.

Stripping out the old headlining

Very careful inspection is required when contemplating the renewal of a headlining. This is always the case when dealing with material that has rotted and is decaying rapidly.

Should this be an unfamiliar task for you, the aid of photographs and drawings prior to stripping out can be invaluable.

Always try to remove the lining as a complete unit, for

The deterioration of this 1951 Ford Mercury headlining is such that great care needs to be exerted if the old lining is to be used as the templates for making the new headlining.
Here the lining is carefully being released from around the rear door aperture

this is where it will be found easiest to make your patterns for the marking and cutting out of the new materials.

Never force headlining fittings, if an area is difficult and doesn't want to budge, ask a friend for advice, for even if he or she has little knowledge of the subject, two heads are always better than one!

The most difficulty is usually found when trying to remove plastic, wood, or metal cappings that have 'concealed' fittings.

A lever in the correct position or sometimes the pushing of the capping in a specific direction assists the release from hidden clips. There are so many fixing methods, that even having been in the panel beating and trimming trade for some 20 odd years I still come across a fixing method not experienced before. So take great care with cappings and mouldings, for their replacement is usually difficult, very often impossible!

Marking out

The majority of headlinings are produced from one length of material, with additions where necessary on each corner and centre. Additions are often required to attach the headlining to the front screen pillars.

Therefore the material length required will be the distance from the front screen to the rear screen, with allowances for each list line and a small amount for stretching into position prior to trimming off. The width of the material is usually large enough to cover the width of the vehicle, but where a very wide roof is contemplated, such as on an Armstrong Siddeley, it may be necessary to calculate the material size in a different manner. See the diagram of marking out of both methods.

Directional pulling

All headlinings, no matter what fabric is used, require a certain 'feel' for their use and in fitting-up require considerable directional pull to ensure that folds and creases do not remain.

If, no matter how hard you have tried, the result is still a number of creases, don't despair. Should these be very prominent, re-position the fabric. Small creases are sometimes inevitable, particularly with the brushed cloth fabrics. When this happens, a process called steaming is

Diagram 5

Wide Headlinings – Showing panels to be joined

Stitch lines – when
complete act as list lines

Stitch lines to join
each headlining panel

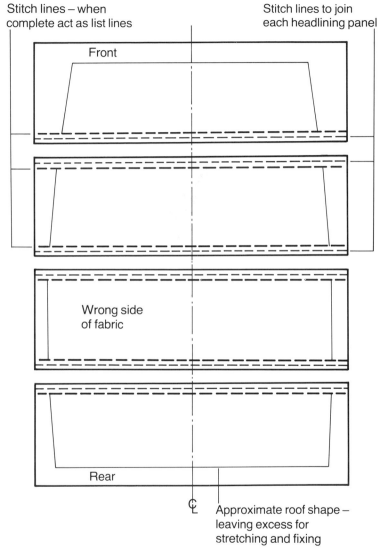

Front

Wrong side
of fabric

Rear

C̸L

Approximate roof shape –
leaving excess for
stretching and fixing

carried out. All that one requires is an electric kettle carefully positioned inside the car (preferably with seats
removed), left to boil, ensuring that windows and doors
are closed.

WARNING: Don't leave the kettle for too long before
inspecting the results, i.e. three to four minutes of full

steam should be sufficient. Check the results making sure that you open the door with care so as not to scald yourself. If creases are starting to disappear, but still remain, give the steaming process a little longer.

3   Problems associated with fitting headlinings, i.e. around sunshine roofs

When a sunshine roof is present, the list bars should be fitted first, then the area surrounding the sunshine roof should be attached with careful stretching out from the centre of each side. Having done this the remainder of the headlining is fitted in the normal manner.

Diagram 6   **Typical Headlining Layout (Average size car)**

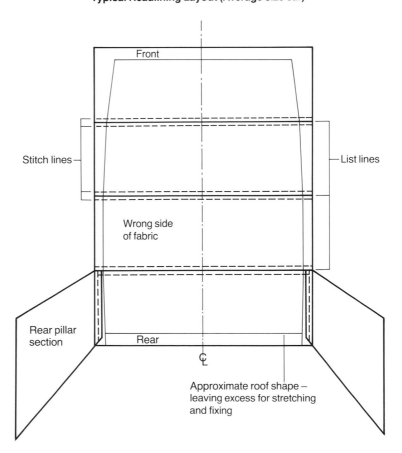

Around courtesy lights and sun visors

The cutting of fabric and fitting of the above are left until the remainder of the headlining has been fitted. These don't normally present a problem except in finding the screw holes for their fittings.

This has to be carefully done with patience using a fine long needle and pushing the lining up against the fitment area to find the screw holes. Should you make a mistake in finding the screw hole there will be no problem; just move the needle from its previous position, incorrect insertion will not be noticeable.

One of the most essential requirements of fitting any trim, is that of keeping the headlining clean. Regular washing of hands prior, and during fitting is essential. One's own clothes must be clean too. Many a headlining has been ruined due to the wearing of dirty overalls and dirty hands.

As a general guide, natural fabrics require longer to steam than do their man-made counterparts.

4   General guidelines for fitment of headlinings

With the headlining ready to fit, check that you are inserting the correct list wire or bar for the relevant list line in the headlining.

Taking care not to puncture the headlining, slide the wires through the list line loops. Gather up the headlining, complete with list bars and position yourself inside the car. (If carpets remain, it pays to cover these with paper or protective sheet in order to avoid soiling them with glue, tools etc.)

Face the front of the car and position the first list bar transversely across the car. Ensure that the list bar is in the upside down position and then 'spring' it into place into the holes provided or alternatively screw each end up with the appropriate fittings. Do this with the remainder of the list bars, gradually making your way to the rear of the car.

All of the headlining should now be temporarily suspended.

Return to the front list bar and twisting through 180 degrees towards the rear of the car, locate the front list bar

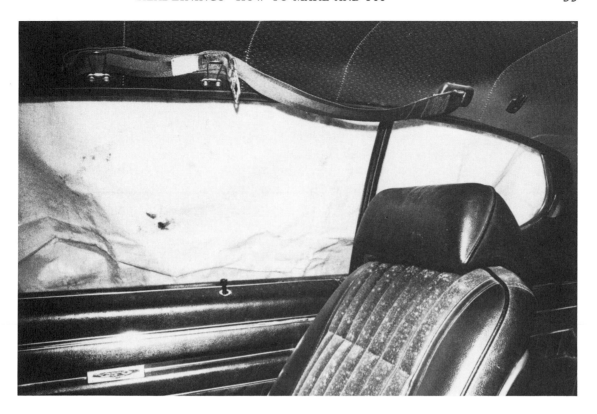

The usual location and fixing point of the passenger's seat belt in this 1969 Pontiac GTO adds to the complexity of replacing such a headlining. Careful labelling of screws and fittings prior to stripping out is essential. The pulling in one direction or another also needs to be considered in relation to this fitment

so that it now follows the contour of the roof. Don't be afraid of using a little excess pressure to spring it into position. The list bar and headlining should be nice and taut, up against a pad stuck to the roof panel itself. Carry on in this same manner for the remaining list bars.

Find the centre of the front of the headlining (previously marked) and line this up with the centre on the front windscreen aperture. (On some cars it will be necessary to remove the windscreens. The rubber seals may fit over the headlining once glued in place.)

Having applied adhesive to both the headlining and windscreen flange, work from the centre outwards glueing in position.

If tacks are to be used, work in a similar manner from the centre outwards. Don't drive the tacks fully home until you have completed the full width and are sure that you are satisfied with the results.

Move to the rear of the car and proceed in a similar manner working again from the centre outwards, making sure that this time you apply considerable tension from front to rear so as to remove any creases between these two points. (There will still be creases remaining that travel from front to rear, but none should remain in a transverse direction.)

Useful hint: To assist with the fixing of the headlining, whether this be by glueing or tacking, bulldog paper clips are a very useful aid whilst pulling fabric into position. You will need something like 20 of these to make life that little bit easier!

The fixing of the sides of the headlining requires a two handed action to remove creases. This is done by pulling, in turn, at either end of each list bar and at the same time smoothing along the list stitch line with the other hand, in a sliding action. The combination of the two i.e. the pulling at the end of the list bar and the smoothing out with the other hand should ensure that *all* creases are removed.

However, don't run into the obvious mistake of pulling too far to one side before pulling in the opposite direction. Please refer to the diagram to ensure that the correct sequence is followed. It is this action of tensioning and smoothing out along the list lines that makes the difference between a professional looking job and a poor attempt. Too much emphasis, therefore, cannot be placed on this aspect.

The fabric to be positioned down the various door pillars is left to last, but again, ensure that tension together with smoothing is carried out before final fixing. This, then, should just leave the trimming off and final fittings of courtesy lights and sun visors etc.

NOTE: No trimming off of what appears to be excess material should be introduced before this point as this always allows for further movement of the fabric should creases be present.

Having decided that all is well, proceed with a sharp knife to cut the remaining residue of fabric away, always making sure that wherever you trim off, will be covered by either the windscreen rubber, door draught excluder rubber, or wooden or plastic fitment to cover up the join between headlining and body panel.

5 Removal and replacement

This 1951 American–built Mercury has a headlining in a typical state of decay and therefore needs great care in its removal in order to ensure that there is sufficient shape left to make templates and patterns for the new headlining.

All fittings such as sun-visors, coat hooks, window surround moulding, etc. need to be removed first, taking care to keep the relative screws with each component. It is often too easy to assume that screws for these fittings all look the same, and indeed their head shape and size may be, but lengths of screws for these fittings vary enormously.

I have often seen this mistake cause real problems, like a screw for a grab handle or sun-visor being too long, screwed up into the component, only to find that when getting out of the car thinking that the job of headlining fitment is complete, that a sharp bump, or even a hole with screw poking through has ruined the paint job; disaster!

It cannot be emphasized enough; log all fittings and screws to avoid this castastrophy.

After removal of fittings the list wires are unclipped from their respective sockets. This view shows the two front list

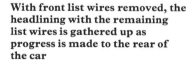

With front list wires removed, the headlining with the remaining list wires is gathered up as progress is made to the rear of the car

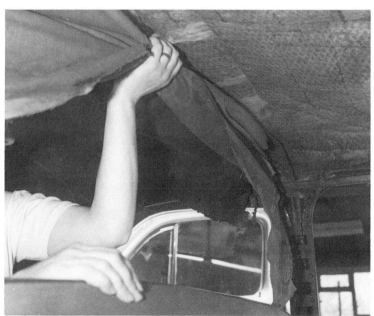

wires removed, the headlining and wires being gathered up as a progression is made towards the rear of the car. Here the complete headlining with list wires is layed out prior to wire removal and subsequently the formation of patterns for the new headliner.

Note that the list wires get progressively deeper in curvature as they get towards the rear of the car.

Before fitting the new headlining, the draught excluder, on this particular vehicle, has to be positioned and fitted.

Two of the old list wires have been temporarily refitted here, just to show their location, which of course cannot normally be seen with the fabric in position. As can be seen, they sit snugly up against the anti-drum felt fixed to the roof.

The insertion of the old list wires or rods needs to be done after ensuring that they are clean and free from rust. Pay particular attention to the position of each wire in relation to its position when fitted to the car.

Now the fitment of the new headlining can commence. Plenty of working area inside the car means the removal of seats, etc. Each list wire is sprung into position and then turned in a backward direction through 180 degrees.

Sun visors also need to be stripped out, but note the comment about different length screws. Always keep the appropriate screws with the fitting being removed. 'Blue Tack' or adhesive tape applied to screws and mounting holes usually works well

Removing the fittings. Here the
rear coat hook is about to be
unscrewed with a Philips
screwdriver.
Each panel that is stitched
together is being suspended by a
list bar

At the rear of the Mercury, the
headlining around the window
will have to be removed. The
flange locating the window
rubber is also the fixing point for
the headlining.
As can be seen, the old lining is
already rotting and falling away,
therefore careful inspection is
necessary before stripping out
commences

With the complete headlining stripped from the car, the making up of the new headlining can commence in earnest. Note how the list bars change in shape and width as the lining stretches rearwards (the rear being supported in the picture)

Now that the old headlining has been removed, the draught excluder requires inspection to determine whether it needs to be replaced, as is often the case. The decision here was easy and the old draught excluder is seen being removed

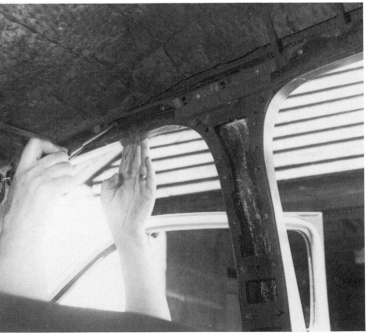

The new draught excluder is being fitted prior to the new headliner. Very often the draught excluder is fitted after the headlining to the pinch weld flange, but the section being used for this Mercury is only acting as a secondary excluder. The primary draught excluder is a rubber section fitted to the door itself

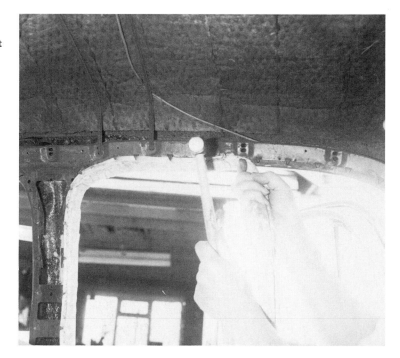

Amazing how fresh the new headlining appears compared to that which was stripped out earlier. Note the use of the old bedspread on the garage floor to ensure the new material remains in a clean condition before fitting

Old list wires or rods are being
inserted into the list loops
stitched as part of the top of the
headlining. Care is required to
ease the rods from one side to the
other, therefore the headliner list
rods must be cleaned and free
from rust

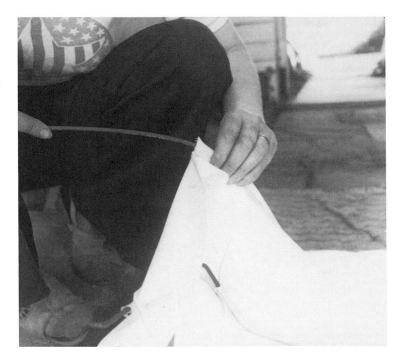

Fitting the new headlining to the
Mercury. Each list rod is being
sprung into its location sockets
and then twisted forwards
through 180 degrees, leaving the
rod to fit neatly and snugly up
against the anti sound deadening
material attached to the roof. In
this case a thick felt is employed

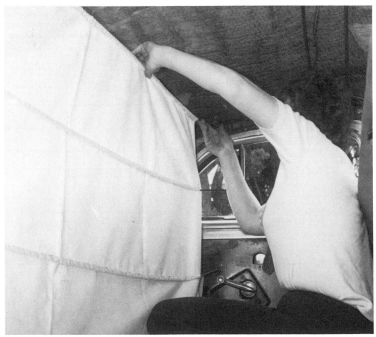

What problems lie in store? The great advantage with this 1932 American Ford limousine is that although very tatty, all the trim components are still there as a guide

A closer view of the 1932 Ford limousine shows the size of the situation. You would be strongly advised to get the professional in for this headlining

Chapter 4 | Seats—Their construction and manufacture of covers

1 The running gear

Slide adjustment mechanisms vary little in their principles of operation from one manufacturer to another, although the actual seat construction determines the details. The better quality the car, the more sophisticated the mechanism is a general rule.

Illustrated is a typical pair of slide adjustment runners, taken from an Alfa Romeo. The ratchet mechanism, as with the great majority of vehicles, operates on just one of these runners and this is the area where the majority of wear and tear takes place, particularly if the vehicle has had many owners or drivers.

Ratchet wear

The wear, if any, will be found in the location of each seat position adjustment hole and on the end of the ratchet lever itself. To overcome this problem, it is necessary to have these worn areas built up with a suitable weld and then carefully filed back to shape. Take care to remove or protect any springs present from the welding process, otherwise the spring tension will be lost and they will have to be replaced.

Distorted units

Apart from worn or dirty units, some seat running gear are prone to distortion. This is due to the runners coming adrift from their mountings in the car floor, either because a bolt has been lost or the floor has become badly split or corroded. Any of these problems puts additional twisting loads on what should remain a pair of parallel seat slide runners.

To overcome distorted slide runners, there is the obvious need to correct the cause of the problem as men-

This driver's seat taken from an Alfa Romeo Spider gives an indication as to many of the problems.

The first thing to note is that the seat is constructed in an unusual manner. It has a tilt back or squab section and this is hinged from about a quarter of the distance along the side of the seat cushion.

Different materials are employed even though they are vinyl finished.

So here is a task requiring new covers to be made, the tilt mechanism needs rebasting, much of the foam needs replacing, and almost certainly, when the seat is stripped down to its pressed steel frame there will be a number of splits that will need welding.

To expect to accomplish this seat as your first 'attempt' would be inadvisable

Both seat runners removed ready for cleaning, light lubrication and identification

tioned before and then tackle the distortion, but avoid the use of a hammer, for this often causes more problems if not used very carefully.

Twisting can be corrected with the aid of a bench vice and an adjustable spanner. One end of the slide carefully clamped in the vice, using spacers if necessary, whilst the adjustable spanner is located on the opposite end and twisted until distortion disappears.

If, however, the slide runner has a bowed type of distortion, then this can be rectified by a squeezing action in the vice with the assistance of three small blocks of wood.

Checking for straightness

This can easily be done with the aid of a 12 in. or 300 mm

Right **Using a bench vice and a
suitably large adjustable
spanner, sufficient in jaw size to
cope with the width of seat
runner, carefully twist back into
position to remove this type of
distortion. Don't overdo it, take a
small amount of movement at a
time and visually check before
de-twisting further**

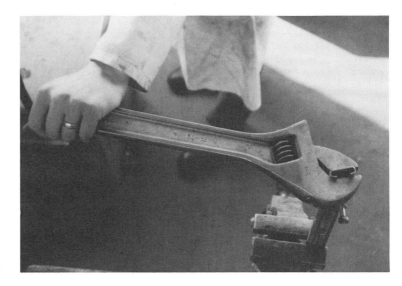

Below **Looking directly over the
straightening situation in the
vice. The main bow here is
approximately two inches from
the end of the adjustment runner**

Above **To remove bow or sag
distortion in a seat adjustment
runner, cut three small pieces of
stout plywood. Place as shown in
bench vice with runner situated
horizontally at the point of
distortion. Gently squeeze the
vice tighter, checking regularly to
measure straightness**

Checking for straightness. Note the gap at the left end of the straight edge whilst checking the distortion of the seat adjustment runner

steel rule, offering up the edge of rule to the seat runner whilst holding both items up to the light. If any significant daylight appears between the two, then obviously further rectification is required. However, if this test is satisfactory, the proof of the pudding, as they say, is to slide one section of the seat runner, the male section inside the female, and see if the action is clean and smooth.

Diagonal checking

Having checked, straightened and cleaned your car seat slide running gear, one further check is necessary. Measure the distance between the mounting point diagonals. If equal, it will prove that the slides are parallel to each other. This latter problem will only be apparent if the car has sustained accident damage or has been poorly repaired around the seat running gear mounting points.

Clevis pin wear

The use of clevis pins will often be found on tilt and slide mechanisms as used in both sports cars and two-door saloons where tilt action to gain access to the rear of the car is required. Clevis pins are held in position by means of a split pin, circlip, rollpin or similar fixing device.

An illustration shows a typically worn clevis pin alongside a new one. These can be readily purchased from garages etc., but state whether the size you require is Imperial or metric.

Cleaning

The most common problem with all seat running gear is that of general dirt and/or carpet fluff clogging up the slides. To remove this foreign matter, soak the runners in a suitable solvent, like paraffin or a mixture of petrol and paraffin, even degreasing fluid, and then with the assistance of an old toothbrush, systematically scrub each slide runner until thoroughly clean. Rinse in fresh solvent, dry off with a dust-free cloth and then apply a small amount of lubricant. Use a lubricant that will not run all over carpets,

Diagram 7

Seat Running Gear – Diagonal checking for squareness

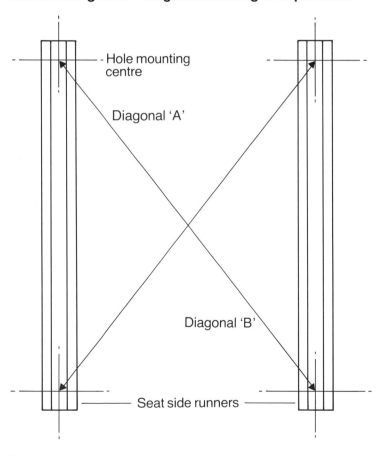

Distances between hole mounting centres must be equal i.e. diagonals 'A' = 'B'

Diagram 8   A common type of clevis pin as used on tilt and slide seat mechanisms

In good condition with
no signs of wear

Badly worn. Replace with new
or if unobtainable, have built
up and re-machined

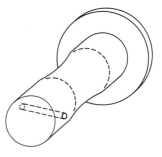

Clevis pins are a very minor detail, but nothing is more annoying than having
just retrimmed the seats, only to find that the passenger seat is merrily rattling
away, simply because of worn clevis pins

It can be appreciated from this
photograph the importance of
having these two independently
mounted passenger seat slides in
which to mount the seat runners
need to be accurately positioned.
This will ensure the smooth
running adjustment of what will
inevitably be for this Bentley S3,
a heavy seat

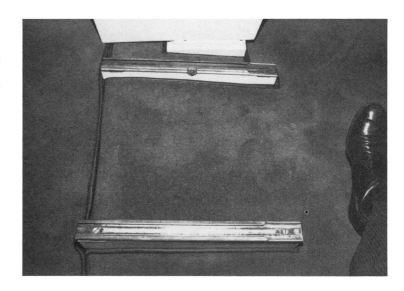

a 'light' type of grease used sparingly will be quite adequate, or to avoid any chance of carpet contamination, use a silicon spray on the seat runners.

2   Frame construction

Seat construction has always been governed by only a few factors. Primarily the type of car; a sports car has entirely different needs to those of a standard sedan or saloon car. The former requires a much lower seat position in relation to the height of the car and the squab needs more lumber support due to the expected high speed cornering from such a car. The standard saloon, however, has the occupants sitting with their knees in a more natural sitting position and the car is expected to travel at more 'sensible' speeds than the sports car. There are often more people in a saloon and some of them could be children!

Having accounted for the basic type of car, there is a secondary but important feature that affects the construction of the seat. The sports car, as with other two-door cars, has to allow for tilting of the complete seat, folding forward of the back of the seat, or a combination of the two. Then there are seats in more luxurious cars that recline, as well as having fore and aft movement. Sometimes those front seats fitted to the very best of vehicles may even have a facility to adjust the seat for height as well.

Hence, all of these facets mean that the construction of the front seats are largely determined by the vehicle type, its quality, and its cost. Despite numerous trials in an attempt to adopt other materials, the tubular steel frame has still proved to be most economical for the strength factors involved.

The most vulnerable seat, of course, will be that of the driver, but the two most significant factors that lead to any and all seat deterioration are those simply attributable to poor seat design and materials first, together with the manner in which the driver and occupants get in and out of the car.

The illustration gives a clear idea of the tilt and fold frame as used in the construction of an MGA seat frame. Note also, that as with almost all car model front seats, each seat is 'handed', i.e., the driver's seat normally has a larger radius curve on the outer edge compared with the smaller curve on the inner edge. Also, the rear section of the seat, known as the squab, is angled with the seat, appearing as though it 'leans' towards the centre of the car.

Consequently, the driver's seat cannot, in most instances, be swapped and fitted into the passenger's side.

Pressed steel

This type of seat construction is a concept that has been with the motor industry for most of its life since birth and did not become superseded by the tubular frame until the

The entry into the rear of this 1940 American Ford coupé demonstrates just how difficult the job is made for the trimmer with the tilt and pivot seat squab

1950s and early 1960s.

Although the seat required less upholstery with a pressed steel frame, it was very heavy and prone to both rust and metal fatigue. A typical seat constructed in this manner is that fitted to the Triumph Spitfire range. Both rust and metal fatigue were most prominent at the base of the seat where it joins the steel pressing of the cushion surround.

Once metal fatigue or corrosion has taken its toll of the steel pressing, which incidentally is only 20 SWG thick (approximately $\frac{1}{16}$ in.), the wired edge is also often affected. The purpose of the wired edge is to give a smooth and substantially increased strength area to a somewhat relatively weak steel sheet. To overcome the weaknesses mentioned, it is necessary to have the splits welded and then it is advisable to reinforce these affected areas with an additional plate of steel. This should be welded to the

A closer view into the Ford coupé gives the impression that with the rear seat squab being very upright and the cushion very short from front to back, that this was designed for 'occasional' use

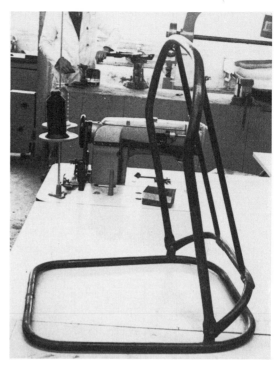

The heart of the matter. A good example of a tilt and fold sports car seat frame prior to being trimmed and upholstered

front face of the squab back section.

In the case of corrosion, the affected area needs to be removed and then replaced with a 'part' panel, with reinforcement if required. The cost of having this repair and reinforcement done professionally is not that expensive. Most fabrication and upholstery shops will undertake the task for something in the region of one to one and a half hours work per seat.

In the accompanying sketch, it can be seen where the seat's reinforcement is positioned. Also shown is its replacement with a part panel over the affected weak area plus the additional reinforcement required to ensure a long lasting repair of what is in effect the most highly stressed area of any car seat.

3 'Making good' repairs—painting, etc.

After welding and reinforcing repairs have been affected, it is necessary to rub down these areas to a suitably good state, i.e. to remove all of the flaky paint, any burnt paint and surface corrosion etc., and then apply a generous coat of red oxide followed by a black gloss.

NOTE: When using red oxide or any other primer, ensure that this will be compatible with the gloss paint. As a general rule, if cellulose gloss is to be applied, always use a cellulose-based red oxide primer. If coach enamel or household paint is to be used, then the red oxide or primer type does not matter.

Allow these paints to dry thoroughly before retrimming the seats.

The significance of this surface pre-treatment after repairs and before trimming will be found invaluable, particularly if adhesives are to be used to attach the primary stuffing to the pressed steel frame. This will ensure good surface adhesion and in turn will allow for the suction of the two surfaces of the stuffing and pressed steel to adhere sufficiently well to ensure a satisfactory, permanent joint.

Diagram 9

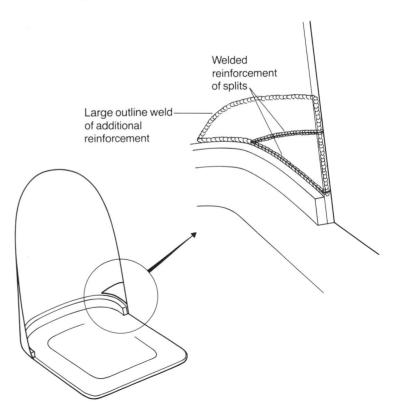

Welded reinforcement of splits

Large outline weld of additional reinforcement

4   Seats—suspension

Three layers of materials make up the basic upholstery of a seat; the cover, the secondary stuffing and the backing fabric. All are then 'suspended' over the seat suspension or frame. This suspension may be achieved by the use of either rubber webbing, coil or Z-springs, a rubber diaphram, compressed composition board or rubber tubes (early 1940s). Some of these suspension methods are easier to replace than others.

Rubber webbing

Often known as Pirelli webbing, this material has the problem of losing its elasticity after many years of use and this results in the seat sagging. Very often the underside of the seat will have evidence of one or more of the strips of webbing having come adrift from the seat frame as well as splitting and fraying around the fixing clips.

If any of these signs are apparent, then the best way is to replace *all* the webbing strips, even if some look in reasonable condition. Failure to do so will mean disappointment, as the remainder of original webbing strips will be weaker than their new replacements, causing unevenness.

To replace webbing seat suspension, all that is necessary

A 1960 Mini seat frame and Pirelli webbing suspension. Necessary tools for fitment are alongside

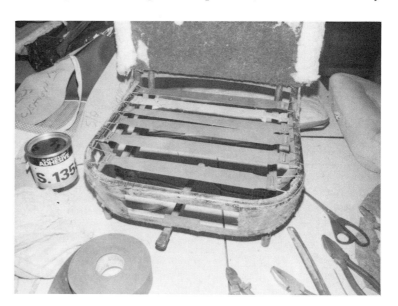

Below **A new spring ready for replacement. These can usually be found in furniture upholsterers' shops as well as some car trimming shops and are relatively inexpensive. Check diameter, thickness or gauge of wire, length and shape for compatibility with the springs that you wish to replace**

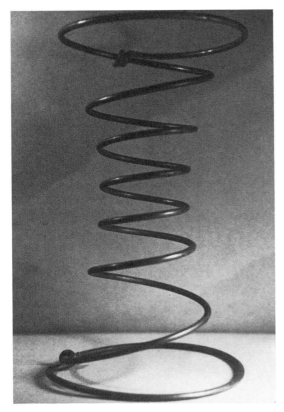

Both above **Two alternative methods of fixing Pirelli webbing to a seat frame. The one on the right is more commonly used, but even this is slightly different from that used for the Mini seat. Nonetheless, this fixing, or that in the top photograph, will suit the Mini style of fitment**

is to calculate the length of webbing required. This can be obtained from your local coach trimmer, hardware shop or furniture upholsterer. The most important thing when purchasing the webbing is to ensure that both the width and thickness is of a similar size to that of the original. The fittings that attach the webbing to the seat frame can usually be used again, but if these are damaged in any way they can be replaced at a cost of a few pence each from the same sources as the webbing.

As for the tension on each webbing strip, this can be to one's own requirements, although normally each strip should be ten per cent short to achieve the proper stretch. This is sufficient to give a reasonably firm suspension to the seat.

Webbing strips vary in length on various parts of the seat, so remember to make a note of their position, or better still, replace one at a time so as to avoid confusion.

Coil springs

Generally speaking, coil springs will not be found very frequently on the cars dealt with in this book; in fact these are to be found, in the main, on car seats of the early 1940s.

However, there are usually three main faults that occur with coil spring seat suspension. The first is lack of tension due to metal fatigue, resulting in the uncompressed spring length being shorter than its original length. Secondly, the spring may be badly affected by rust, either because of the poor state of the vehicle generally or through heavy condensation, and thirdly, the spring may have broken.

Whichever cause of spring weakness or failure, the replacement is the only solution. Ensure that the correct length, diameter, shape and wire gauge is employed.

The cost of the average spring is low so this is not the problem. Actual fixing of the replacement coil spring will often be the biggest difficulty. Springs were often assembled onto the spring frame by machine and because of this, one's ingenuity has to prevail in the compromise for a method of hand assembly. Whether you use wire, assisted by pliers, or carefully re-use the original fittings, the significant thing to remember is that the spring, when fitted properly, should not twist and revolve through the fixing points. Should this be allowed to happen, it will result in the spring cutting its way through the secondary stuffing and eventually through the cover itself.

Sinuous or snake springs

(Proprietary brands: Z- or zig-zag springs

These springs were invented to supersede coil springs and their introduction was for the purpose of speeding up mass production and thus reducing cost. It is for these reasons that any problems associated with Z–springs normally mean that repair or replacement is more difficult to effect. This doesn't mean that the springs can't be obtained, rather that their fitting is made difficult due to automated manufacturing techniques.

Having said this, if you are prepared to be patient and don't mind painstakingly unpicking machine-clamped clips so that they can be re-used, then repairs can be effected quite successfuly.

The problems that apertain to coil springs also affect Z–springs in just the same manner, so investigate for similar faults. The only difference being, that when a Z–spring needs replacing, the whole strip has to be removed and replaced by new.

Rubber diaphrams

These were often used on Rootes Group cars and their advantage, both in production and replacement, is that they are so easy to remove and refit. This is simply a matter of removing the clips securing the cover to the frame, lifting off the foam and then unclipping each spring clip from the seat frame to diaphram in turn.

The reason for needing to replace the rubber diaphram is that splitting, caused by wear and tear or rubber perishing, occurs around the metal reinforcement areas from which the suspension clips are fixed.

Replacement is the only method to cure the problem. Should this not be possible due to the diaphram being unobtainable as a replacement part, then there are two alternatives. The first is to try and locate a suitable second-hand replacement from a breaker's yard, or if all else fails, then the seat will have to be converted to webbing suspension.

To be able to convert to webbing it is necessary to drill the seat frame to accommodate the webbing clips. The

Diagram 10   Rubber diaphragm seat base. Size and shape may vary considerably as well as the number of attachment points to the seat frame

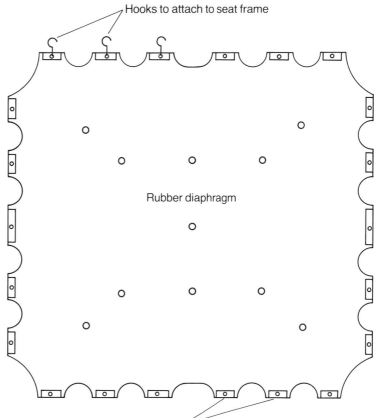

Hooks to attach to seat frame

Rubber diaphragm

Metal reinforcement blocks moulded into rubber. Most splits will occur adjacent to these blocks

webbing spacings need to be such that each gap is approximately two thirds the width of the webbing. This means that for the average seat, you will require five strips of webbing and ten clips and fittings.

Compressed composition board

This method of seat support was a 'new' mass production process that was innovative but then didn't appear to 'catch on'. The BMC/BL 1100/1300 Hydrolastic range were one of the few models to adopt this type of seat construction. It consisted of a tubular frame to which was attached a shaped, one-piece compressed board. The method of attachment was by means of $\frac{3}{16}$ in. diameter pop rivets and washers.

The seat suspension was derived simply by the thick foam that was stuck to this shaped board, but it was the compressed board that led to its failure. Very often the board would crack and disintegrate.

The repair of such compressed board seat supports can be effected by a fibreglass matting and resin repair. One can even renew the whole composite board by using the moulded shape as a mould for its fibreglass replacement, but this would only be necessary if the majority of the composition is in a poor state.

To repair with fibreglass, simply cut some pieces of chopped stranded matting sufficiently large to cover the split or hole, overlapping either by at least another 3 in. all round. Mix-up some resin and activator (hardener) and with the aid of a brush, stipple the resin mix through each layer of matting as it is layed over the repaired area. Three layers of matting should give sufficient strength. If any of the repairs are on the edge of the seat frame, the fibreglass repair can be drilled to enable re-fixing to the frame.

5   Inflatable rubber tubes

The inflatable seat does present some unusual problems. This type is normally only found on vehicles of the early part of the collectable period covered in this book, i.e. 1940s.

Common faults associated with this method of seat upholstery suspension are mainly connected with the deterioration of the rubber, often due to deflation and lack of maintenance. Deterioration causes the rubber carcass to crack, crumble, and generally disintegrate. On the other hand, the cause of the deflation may be as simple as a puncture, easily rectified in the normal manner with a puncture repair kit.

However, if the former is the case, then steps have to be taken to renew a section or number of sections of the rubber tubing. Your local tyre depot near at hand will be the best place to look for assistance, or the classified advertisements in one of the specialist car restoration magazines, may also have what you require.

The important point, wherever the repairs are carried out is to obtain tubing of the correct diameter and then have it cold vulcanized together with what is going to be reclaimed out of the old inflatable seat.

Cold vulcanization is simply the action of using a cleansing solution on the area to be repaired or joined, roughed up with some emery or rubbing down paper, dusting off and then applying vulcanizing solution to both surfaces. Allow time for solution to become touch dry, and then bring both surfaces together, adding plenty of pressure. Dust off the vulcanized area with French chalk, and then inflate ready for testing by immersing in clean water.

6 The use of foam

Foam has been used as a seat suspension material throughout the postwar period, although in the early years and up to the late 1950s to early 1960s this was a rubber–based foam, usually Dunlopillo foam rubber or something similar.

In the latter half of this period however, the introduction of cheap polyurethane foam made these 'old' materials too expensive, and also the 'new' foam was usually more easily moulded to shape in mass production techniques.

The close-up of this seat shows it in a poor state of collapse with the moulded polyurethane foam bursting through the worn cover. It is seats having complex shapes such as this that enabled poly-foams to be more economically viable compared with Dunlopillo foams.
However, one of the disadvantages of poly-foams is that it is more susceptible to crumbling than Dunlopillo type foam once open to the wear and tear of the seat occupant

Using polyurethane foam as a secondary stuffing, the leather cover is here being stitched through the foam and backing fabric, in this case calico is being used

Dunlopillo foam rubber needed a stronger suspension of springs, usually of the coil type, whereas the more modern foams being denser, needed less rigid support. It was undoubtedly the introduction of the new foams that led to a change in seat construction, and it was at approximately the same time that the Z–springs were introduced on a mass production scale.

Although the Z–springs offer less support in an 'opposing' or upward direction to the occupant of a seat, its linear strength meant it was far more effective than coil springs. It was the use of the polyurethane foam that also meant the need for different methods of attachment, hence the introduction of a mass of new adhesives.

WARNING: Take care when using adhesives. There are three good reasons for this:

1 Most modern adhesives have a low flash point and therefore have a high fire risk.
2 Ensure that the adhesive is applied in a 'free' atmosphere with plenty of fresh air. This is to avoid being overcome by fumes.
3 And most important from the point of the job in hand, make sure that the adhesive is compatible with the foam to be fixed. Failure to do so may result in the adhesive melting the foam after a period of time.

Rubber latex foam

This type of foam is constructed by encasing numerous interconnecting air cells with pure rubber latex. Compared with polyurethane foam it is more expensive and consequently is no longer used in the mass produced car. Rather, it is confined to public service vehicles and some luxury cars where the accent is on longevity and durability.

The cushions for vehicle seats in our period were produced in metal moulds, the degree of support being governed by a number of factors. As with any type of foam, the density is very significant. Secondly, the size and shapes of the cushion unit together with the space of the internal cavities also give varying results with regard to seat support.

Large cavities within the latex foam produce a softer feel, whereas smaller cavities give firmer support. The latter type is, therefore, used for the surrounding areas of the seat cushion. When working with latex foam one experiences a pleasant substance to work with. It is a product that is not prone to mildew, vermin, moths etc.

Polyurethane foam

The choice of foam should be governed by three characteristics: density, hardness and thickness. It is also worth noting that latex foam compresses very evenly in respect of increasing pressure, whereas polyurethane foam demonstrates an initial resistance and then tends to collapse to almost its full depth or thickness. This 'collapsing' is often reduced by the surround of the seat cushion being made of foam chips held together by liquid foam and machined to shape.

Foam density of conventional polyurethane foams is calculated by weight ratio, i.e., 1 lb per cu. ft to 3 lb per cu. ft. For the seat squab, i.e., the back rest, densities from 1 to 1.5 lb per cu. ft are adequate. The latter are only suitable for non-load bearing areas. The seating cushion requires a density of 1.8 lb per cu. ft, and above. The higher the density the better and therefore the likelihood of greater comfort.

Selection and cutting of foam

It is unlikely that one can purchase a ready-made moulded

cushion for a particular vehicle of this period. Consequently, it will be necessary to purchase the foam in slab form and cut to size and shape accordingly.

The cutting will be made easier by adopting one of the following suggestions:

1 The use of a fine–toothed hacksaw blade.
2 A long sharp kitchen or carving knife.
3 An electric carving knife.
4 A pair of strong, large scissors dipped in water.

When measuring up for size, always allow approximately half an inch extra all round in order that the cover will fit really snugly.

An important point to remember when fitting latex foam, particularly a rear seat cushion mounted to a plywood base, is to ensure that a number of air release holes are drilled in the plywood. This enables the air to escape when the cushion is sat on. Failure to do this will result in a very hard and uncomfortable seat.

7   Secondary stuffings

This is the term given to the materials used immediately underneath the seat cover and which may take the form of horse hair, coconut hair, Lintus felt, cotton waste, foam, plus many derivatives of these substances.

The purpose of these stuffings is primarily to give the cover fabric its shape and aesthetic appearance and as a secondary measure to give additional comfort to the overall suspension of the seat. Secondary stuffings also reduce the wear that may take place between the seat frame and the cover fabric. Very often these stuffing materials are attached in part to the cover as is the case with flutes.

The necessity with any of these stuffings, apart from horse hair, is to replenish with new. Horse hair, on the other hand, is always re-usable, provided it is cleaned first. The easiest way to achieve this is to put the old horse hair into something like an old pillow case, tie the top and put the complete bundle into the washing machine, put it through the relevant cycle and then tumble dry. Not only does this clean the hair but it puts the spring and bounce back.

Bench seats in the front of cars are difficult to find in such good order as in this 1940 Chevrolet. The brushed velour cover and neatly double stitched corners are a pleasure to look at. The fittings ie, the screws, adjustment lever are all original and these are complemented by the velour trim panel and door furniture. A smooth seat such as this without flutes, borders etc. needs considerable skill in order that any bumps or hollows do not show in the finished product

8 Covers

Don't forget that to attempt the making-up of seat covers, it is necessary to have access to an industrial sewing machine. However, even if this is not possible it is useful to know how this technique is carried out in order that when you decide to have your car seats retrimmed, you will be better equipped to choose the material and method of assembly as well as be able to talk in a more relaxed manner to your local trimmer.

Materials

There are generally three layers of material employed in the upholstery and covering of car seats postwar and up to approximately 1970.

The cover itself can be made of many things. The majority are listed in chapter 1.

Underneath the cover is the substance known as second-

The interior of this Jaguar XK120 almost allows us to smell the copious amounts of leather employed in this unique trimming exercise. However, if inexperienced, seek the professional for his advice and pay for his expertise, for the skill required here warrants some years of experience

A classic example where it is not necessary to replace a complete seat with new leather. Apart from the tear in the lower left of the picture of this Jensen driver's seat which will require a replacement panel, the remainder can be readily rejuvenated by the Connollizing process.
The cost of such a process is very moderate in comparison to leather recovering

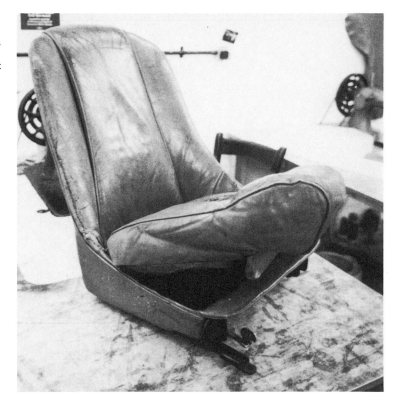

ary wadding, polyurethane foam or equivalent substance. To hold this secondary stuffing in place, a layer of calico is most commonly used.

Leather

The use of leather for the covering of car seats has been with the car industry since its inception and still remains one of the most sought after options, even in the modern motor car. With its 'natural' talent to breathe and be cool to sit on in the summer, yet warming up very quickly in winter, it has been difficult to replace with any man-made alternative.

If the vehicle that you are contemplating renovation on has leather upholstery, do not immediately assume that because it appears cracked and worn that it has to be replaced. Very often these problems can be readily overcome with what is known as re-Connollizing. Obviously, if there are splits and gaping holes in various parts of the seats, then these will have to be replaced by new leather, but normally this can be confined to one or two pleats or panels.

Connolly Brothers Ltd offer an excellent service to rejuvenate any car's leather upholstery and this is des-

Diagram 11   The layout of a leather hide prior to cutting

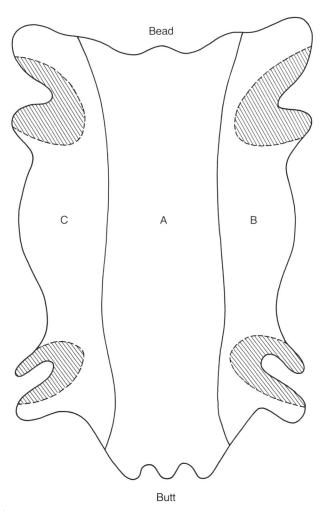

The centre section 'A' is the heaviest area with fibres growing in all directions: Side sections 'B' and 'C' also have fibres growing in all directions but are much lighter, hence these are used for areas in the car that receive relatively light amounts of wear, such as door and quarter trim panels. Those areas that are shaded are called the flank areas and should only be used where there is no wear or flexing as the fibres only grow in one direction

The following six shots are some of the faults that the leather currier has to deal with and as much as possible avoid the purchase of. However, some of these faults may still be found on a new hide, albeit on a small scale. It is because of these faults, some natural, some not, that the selection and cutting of a new hide requires thorough planning to make the optimum use.

In this first photo, the warble fly has eaten its way under the skin leaving what are known as 'pot' marks

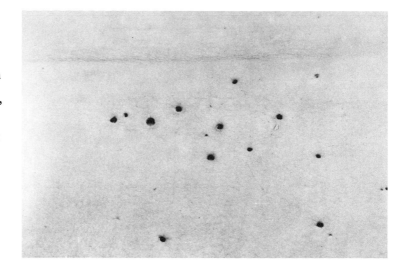

The effect of barbed wire and the healing process together with old age are the causes for this tough and certainly not very supple hide

cribed in detail in Peter Wallage's book, *How To Restore Car Interiors*. Thus, seek advice before you decide to refurbish or replace, after all, there is a significant difference in cost.

Assuming that you decide to replace the leather, and this will often be necessary when a car has been open to the weather for some time, then take your seats to an expert. For unless you have tackled any upholstery before, it is expensive as and when you make mistakes. Leather is not

Little can be done with this serious fault apart from cut round it Barbed wire is the cause of these deep abrasions that have since healed and left deep scars

Brand marks are becoming rare in some parts of the world as this wastes usable hide. More producers are moving towards a disc attached to the ear lobe. This brand mark if viewed from the individual straight line is not just the letter 'S' but depicting the symbol of a swan

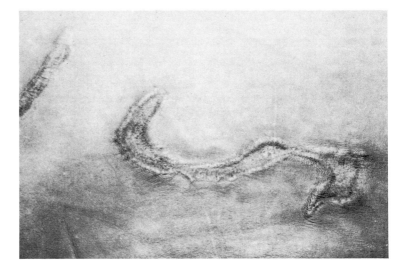

an easy substance to work with and requires a high degree of skill.

Should you feel confident enough, the techniques for marking out, cutting, stitching, etc., are virtually the same as for any other fabric. The only significant differences are the selection of various parts of the hide to make optimum use of them. Also the stitch length is very important. Too many stitches to the inch and the leather will be cut as fast

Numerous faults on the surface of this hide make it unusable, but these imperfections will not be found over the whole hide. The majority of the square footage of hide will be easily usable, but this does reduce the scope and size of the products that can be produced.

The line running across the centre of the picture is almost certainly an 'age' line, whilst the pain of opposed triangular shapes in rubbing up against barbed wire, but this time in a vertical up and down movement.

The bad abrasion at bottom right was probably caused by a protruding nail

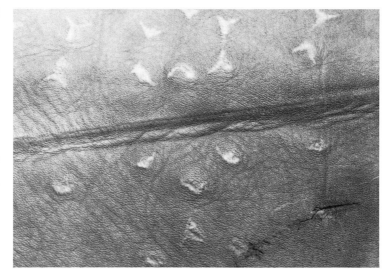

Work done by the individual who flails the hide of the carcass has caused these marks on what was a perfectly good hide. Probably the work of an apprentice or trainee

as it is stitched. Depending on fitment, eight to ten stitches per inch is ample to ensure a strong seam without the risk of cutting through the leather.

9 Patterns
Marking out and cutting

Once you have made the decision to make your own seat covers and chosen the various materials, the process of

Having removed the side plates further damage to the cover is apparent! Take these hidden and very often expected defects for granted and then allowances can be made in your original estimate of costs to be incurred

The close-up of the split in the vinyl cover of this Alfa Romeo Spider 1300 Junior seat may look an easy task, but the contruction of the seat is such that considerable skill is required to take on such a task.
The squab section of the seat pivots from the lower swivel of the side fixing plate. So the first thing to accomplish is the removal of both side plates to separate the squab from the cushion

marking-out has to be investigated.

Whenever possible, the old cover should be used as the guide to work to. The fluted or pleated cushion (the part that is sat on) should be unstitched from the border and piping. Likewise, the seat back needs to be unstitched, allowing the front and back sections to be laid out flat. This will enable you to mark round the shapes carefully for your patterns on the new materials.

The width of the flutes is very important and the measurement for these differs from one vehicle manufacturer to another. A common finished width on the cover material is 2 in., but this requires a pre-stitched width of $2\frac{1}{2}$ in., leaving $\frac{1}{2}$ in. for seam allowances. The calico backing, however, is marked out using the finished flute width of 2 in.

Diagrams showing the method for marking out the pattern on both the cover and the calico can be found near this text.

As for the cutting, (apart from the overall sizes that you commenced with), leave this until *all* the stitching on the cushion has been completed. The cutting for the shape of the seat is left until *after* the secondary stuffing has been added, no matter which method of seat cover manufacture you choose to adopt.

Right **The metal tabs retaining the upholstery to the pressed steel base are now levered up**

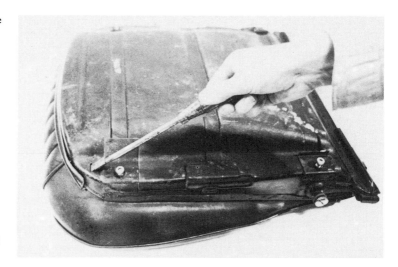

Both below **With metal tabs released, the seat cushion is lifted out and away from the base**

Stripping the cover from the seat squab base of this Alfa Spider seat will take about half an hour. This needs to be done to obtain the cover for pattern purposes. A set of Allen keys is necessary, in this instance metric, to be able to remove the seat runner adjusters. The two Allen keys screws at the rear of the upturned seat are being released first. Adjusters will then be slid back to remove the remaining Allen screws at the front of the seat squab and having turned the seat through 180 degrees it now reveals the pressed steel base on

the left with the polyurethane moulded foam support situated inside the cover fabric. The whole assembly on the right of the

picture is held together with a relatively flimsy pressed steel frame to which the cover fabric is attached with the aid of hog rings

Here, some of the seat cover components have been carefully unpicked at the seam. This is done more easily by clamping one part of the seat cover under the clamp foot of the sewing machine adjacent to a seam. Pull the next seat panel away from the clamp foot and simultaneously cut with scissors or knife along the stitched seam. Move work under clamp foot as necessary to progress along each seam. Using this method, the sewing machine clamp foot acts like another hand.

Note also that each seat panel template has been marked. This is particularly helpful in speeding things up when it comes to the machining aspect. It is a must when stripping and matching covers for a pair of seats in order to avoid confusion and create mistakes

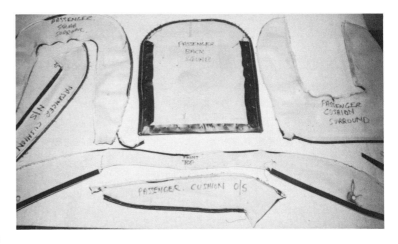

Stitching machining

The first line of machining is taken at one end (see diagram) of both fabrics or the line nearest to the centre and it is at this point that the method and material used for the stuffing will determine the sequence of events.

Method A: As used on most collectable vehicles in the late 1950s and 1960s. This is normally recognized as the easiest method, using foam as the secondary stuffing material.

Having marked out the calico and then, the cover on the

'wrong' side of the material, lay the calico on the sewing machine bench with the flute marks uppermost. Mark the foam sheet in a similar manner to the calico i.e., on the finished side of the flutes. Lay it also with the flute marks uppermost and with the cover material folded back to the first stitch line (see photograph). Lay this over the appropriate stitch line on the foam with a quarter of an inch overlap.

With all three pieces of material; the calico, foam and cover in alignment, place in *front* of the sewing machine foot, sliding in position for the first stitch (always ensuring that the needle is at the top of the stroke). Clamp the work-

Situated on the back of the vinyl material are the patterns. These have been marked with a felt tip marker pen with the old panels as templates. Make sure that the templates are layed out with the face side downwards.
The outline of each pattern is the cutting line, whereas lines situated ½ in. inside the cut line is that marked for stitching/seam allowance

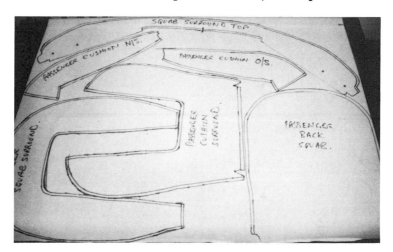

Patterns cut to size and ready for the stitching assembly.
I have included here on the cushion surround panel, shown in the centre of the picture, a piece of vinyl with a fault line in full view. This sort of fault is quite a common occurrence and needs to be investigated before purchasing the vinyl. Nothing's worse than thinking that you have every thing prepared, only to find that more material has to be purchased and the piece marked out and cut again.
So always inspect the material, whatever it happens to be and make allowances for any faults present

Diagram 12

The diagrams here are those necessary when marking out for a rear seat squab section. If the seat is extra wide you can join the fabric on any one of the stitch flute lines without any problem, as long as the nap etc is flowing in the same direction.

Should you want to make up front seat covers, the same principles apply, just modify the number of flutes and width of border to suit your car's requirement.

It is very important to get the first and second flute stitch line carried out accurately to ensure that everything remains parallel. Should you find that this is not very satisfactory, undo the stitches and start again

Marking out the pattern ready for stitching. The numbers represent stitch line sequence.   'A' = fabric face side   'B' = calico face side

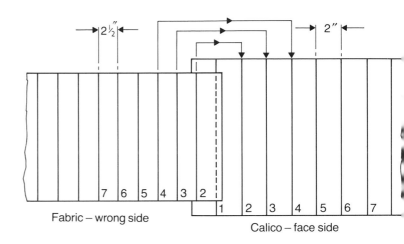

Fabric – wrong side

Calico – face side

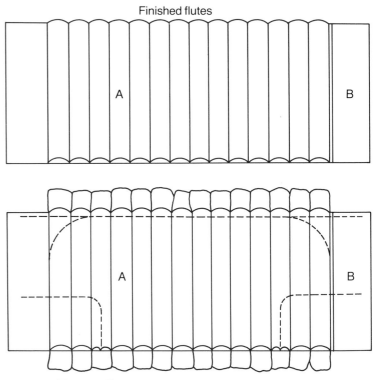

Finished flutes

A   B

A   B

Flutes stuffed – border stitched – ready for trimming off

Using tailor's chalk and a good long straight edge, the flutes are marked on the wrong side of the cover fabric with the face side downwards on to the bench. This particular material is a brushed nylon on a cotton backing coloured black

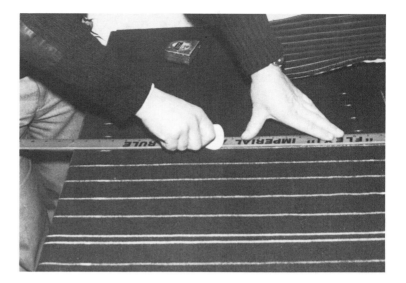

The two stitch lines have been completed here to produce the first 'flute'. Leather is the cover fabric being employed, a beautiful medium to work with together with that unmistakable aroma!

piece with the foot of the machine and proceed to stitch all three fabrics.

When this first stitch run is complete, stop the machine, bring the needle to the top of the stroke, lift the clamp foot and draw the workpiece out from the *rear* of the machine. This reduces the risk of the thread snagging up. Allow enough thread to run free (approx 6 to 8 in.), cut off thread with scissors *adjacent* to the workpiece.

Stitching the first machine line. It is sometimes preferable, as with the small number of flutes involved in this seat cover, to commence as near as possible to the centre of the work piece. This can, however, if not careful, make the centre flute rather narrow. When starting at one end of the workpiece and progressing with each flute to the other end there is no chance of this happening

Having stitched the fluted centre section of the cushion cover, the border edge is now being passed through the stitch line of the machine from right to left of the picture. Note that the backing fabric and foam are not trimmed to size, this will be done when the stitching of this stage has been completed. This gives the advantage of being able to hold the workpiece square to the sewing machine table in order to assist with steering the work through the machine and therefore making it easier to keep the flutes true and parallel

You should now have the start of a successful seat cover! Proceed to the next adjacent stitch line, working outwards, folding the top cover back to the left each time prior to stitching.

Method B: This is the traditional method employed on the earlier cars using cotton wadding *after* the stitching of flute lines.

The marking out of the wrong side of the cover and the calico is carried out in the *same* manner as Method A, but without the interlayer of foam.

Proceed in a similar fashion, with the stitching of the two materials. The stuffing, however, is placed in position after machining and this can be done with the aid of what is known as a stuffing stick.

The cotton wadding (or alternative material) is cut to size. You will find that in most cases, the wadding will tear

Carefully marking out the reverse or wrong side of the cover material. The need for accuracy here is very apparent for this is your only guide when the material is passing rather rapidly past the sewing machine needle. You can make your own useful marking out rule, similar to the one shown here. It can either be wood or as in this case a strip of metal.

To speed up the marking out, a number of divisions are placed at regular intervals along the straight edge i.e., one inch at a time. These can be cut carefully with a small hacksaw and it is surprising how much use will be made of these divisions, rather than keep picking up a straight edge and a tape measure every time

New and old. The stripped parts of the cushion of this 25-year-old Austin Mini seat shown on the right demonstrates how much the seat has worn, faded and eventually torn rather badly. The new cover at the top of the pictures has brought all the colour back and this together with the flute stuffed in the traditional manner gives the cover that sumptuous look. Originally, the flutes were manufactured using the electrical welded seam method, but if you wish to make these up yourself the traditional method is one alternative or you will have to take the material to your local trimmer that has a resistance heat weld machine for vinyl fabrics.

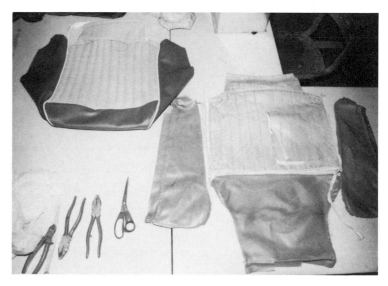

Stuffing of flutes using method 'B' (traditional). The left hand is in position to retain the end of the 'open' flute whilst the right hand is gripping the 'stuffing' stick loaded with a length of cotton wadding

Having started the insertion of stuffing stick and wadding, the left hand now changes to the underside of the job and grips firmly the calico backing. With a steady pressure, push the stuffing stick through to the opposite end of the flute, but make sure that a short length of wadding is left showing

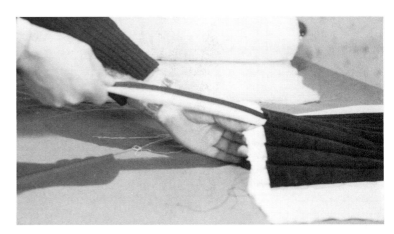

Whilst holding on to the wadding with right hand (protruding at the start of the flute), carefully pull the stuffing stick strap through the opposite end

Finally, still holding on to the wadding with right hand, pull the stuffing stick completely out of the flute, leaving the cotton wadding in position as required. This sequence is then continued until all flutes are stuffed

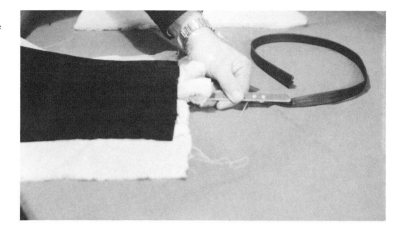

along the roll but requires scissors to cut across the roll. Tearing gives the advantage that when the wadding is rolled into a tube prior to being placed in each flute, there will be no hard defined edge protruding and then noticed through the cover.

Wadding strips need to be 4 to 5 in. longer than the flutes, but the width, prior to being rolled into a tube, is entirely up to your individual requirements. As a guide, three times the width of flute is usually adequate, but obviously if you require a very dominant shape to the flute then the wadding will need to be rolled to a thickness of 4 or 5 times that of the flute. Likewise if you require a very 'flat' flute, then reduce the number of thicknesses.

To insert the wadding, roll or fold the wadding across the narrow width for the desired number of times, e.g. three. Open the stuffing stick strap, fold the wadding over the end of the stick and clamp in place with the strap. You should now be able to hold the wadding and stuffing stick in one hand. Holding the end of the cover fabric in one hand, proceed to slide the stuffing stick up and through one of the flutes. With 2 or 3 in. protruding at the opposite end of the flute, retain the solid part of the stick with one hand, whilst pulling the strap out at the other end. Finally, carefully pull out the complete stuffing stick, ensuring that the cotton wadding remains in position. Carry on with remaining flutes and you will notice that the depth obtained from the top fullness of the flute to the bottom

To the right of the picture, the flutes have all been stuffed with cotton wadding and the piping machined in position. The view on the left shows the flutes with all the excess stuffing, calico etc. cut away, except the lower section which is left until much later. This means that this seat centre section is now ready to be stitched to the border

The vinyl border being stitched to the centre fluted section. The line marked on the back of the vinyl border is the stitch line and this is $\frac{1}{2}$ in. from the edge of the material. It is still necessary at this stage to continue with the piping clamp foot, for this is already in position on the same seam

stitch line area is more satisfying generally to the eye than the previous method described (using the foam as a secondary stuffing).

Having used either the foam or the cotton wadding and completed the fluted sections, it remains to stitch the shapes for the edge of the seat prior to adding the piping and surrounding materials. This is simply a matter of fol-

The leather cover for a Bentley S3 front seat squab, ready for final stitching having been fluted and stuffed in the traditional manner

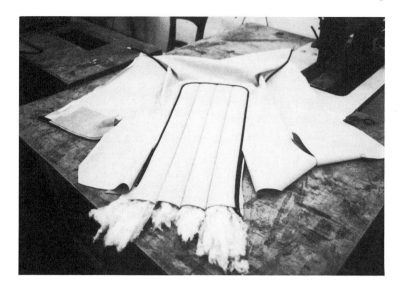

To recreate the vinyl welded seams as on the driver's seat of this 1967 Pontiac GTO, it is necessary to acquire the service of a vinyl weld machine, otherwise an alternative method, i.e., the traditional will have to be considered

lowing the line of the pattern with the sewing machine. The only difficulty here is dealing with both the very thick to very thin substances as the machine passes over the flutes. To assist, it may be necessary from time to time to lift the foot on the machine to assist the passage of the fabric past the needle.

The piping is machined on the same stitch line as the

Could the trim lines on any vehicle look more crisp or magnificent than this? The contrasting piping adds that classic touch

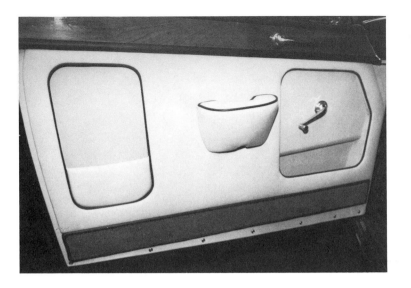

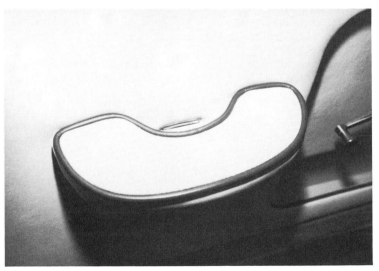

pattern line. (See the illustrations). The border is then placed face to face with the seat squabs with $\frac{1}{2}$ in. left for border, and machined in position.

NOTE: The machining of the piping to the squabs and the border to the squabs is much easier to achieve with the aid of a piping foot.

Should the seats that you want to restore have welded

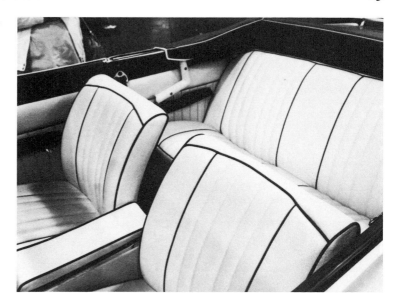

This heavy grained cream vinyl is edged with a black contrasting piping. It's personal choice as to whether this is slightly 'overdone' compared with the Bentley S3 seats. However, this retrimmed vehicle is as near as possible to the original specification and this is what is most important
Note the absence of any joins in the piping cover material. To achieve this and in particular with the rear seat, allowance for considerable wastage must be contemplated, unless of course more than one vehicle of the same type is being envisaged for retrimming. For the rear seat squab a length of material for piping would need to be in the region of 120 in. in length. Therefore this would have to be taken from the length of material as the width of 48 or 54 in. is insufficient without joining

seams (as those of many cars of the 1960s had) then there is little to be achieved without the aid of a machine capable of welding plastic or vinyl materials. To achieve this sort of originality you will have to buy either ready-made replacements or take the necessary materials to a trimming shop which can tackle such a job—most should be able to.

Incidentally, the welding machine bonds the cover material (e.g. the vinyl) through the foam secondary stuffing to the stockinette or calico backing. Therefore, you will also need all of these items prepared prior to the trimmer engaging his welding machine.

Having got your welded seams completed, the piping and border are stitched on in just the same manner as the seat squabs with stitched flutes.

10　Piping

Plastic piping can be bought readily from most trimming shops, but if your vehicle's seats have a complimentary piping, whether the same material and/or colour as the seat cover, or a contrasting colour, then the making up is readily done on the sewing machine. To do this easily, a piping foot is required.

The cover material needs to be approximately 1 in. wide.

Although rear seats may appear to be a daunting task, generally they are just an extension in width of the principles involved in front seat manufacture. However, the frame construction may differ considerably, but I don't expect you to 'have a go' at this type of seat as fitted to a 1964 S3 Bentley, for it is all leather covered in off-white hide with contrasting black piping. A unique example of Connolly Brothers' trimming department

The length of material obviously needs to be the desired length for the seat in question and this often requires the need for a join. Joins should either be placed in unobtrusive positions or, as in the case of the back of a seat or a long bench seat, a join is unavoidable and therefore must be placed centrally.

To achieve this join with the minimum of bulkiness and maximum strength, the cover material for the piping needs to be marked out as in the pattern shown.

Once the necessary joins have been made in the cover material, the piping cord is placed along its length, folded over and placed under the piping foot, ready for machining.

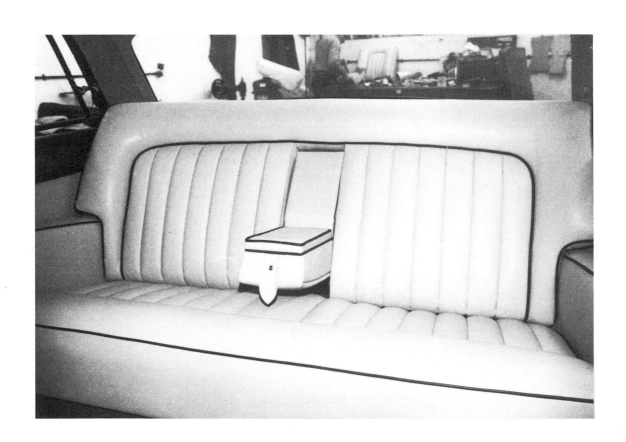

Left **Piping cord by the reel. You need not buy this much of course, but it does work out cheaper. Your local trimmer will supply it by the metre**

Above **Detail trimming, as on this matching arm rest, is very important from the point of view of overall look**

11 Fitment of covers

With the cover turned inside out and commencing with the front of the seat (it makes no difference whether this is a single front seat or a long front or rear bench seat) position the corner of the cover over the corner of the upholstery. In this case the cover is leather and the upholstery is foam.

Positioning the second front corner

The second front corner, note the pulling with the right hand of the seam to ensure the top of the seat cushion remains free from additional fabric thickness

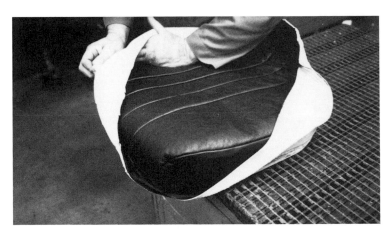

With front corners of the black leather covered seat cushion in position it remains to carry out the same procedure on the rear of the cushion. Careful smoothing out as the remaining corners are pulled is necessary to ensure that creases can slide over the clinging surface of the foam

Fixing the staples. Note the position of the seat in order to be able to view and grip the leather to take into account the shape, crease etc. that need to be eliminated

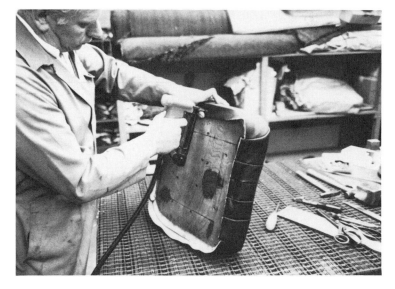

Having positioned the cover over one of the front corners, ensure that the allowance for seam is pulled out and downwards. Position the left hand inside the cover over the corner and press down firmly. With the right hand, proceed to pull the cover down and over the corner.

Continue with the opposite front corner, again ensuring that the allowance for the seam is pulled out and downwards. Carry out the same procedure for the rear of the seat, smoothing out the cover from the centre outwards where necessary.

**The completed leather covered
driver's seat cushion with
polyurethane foam as the
secondary stuffing and
Dunlopillo foam as the main
suspension situated on a plywood
baseboard.
It should see many years of
service as long as fed correctly at
regular intervals to avoid drying
out and cracking etc**

This particular seat has a plywood mounting board and is therefore ideal for the use of a staple gun. The gun used here is a pneumatic one and care must be taken not to accidentally fire the trigger until ready for use. As for fixing the leather cover around the base board, stand the seat on edge so that when stretching the leather in position with one hand and the staple gun ready in the other, one is able to see at the same time the position and tension prior to firing in the staple.

Opposite sides are temporarily stapled first and then progress is made along each side and around each corner, ensuring that no creasing takes place, except on the underside of the seat where this is permissible. The same technique can be achieved with a manually operated staple gun (as shown in the tools section) although it will take a little longer.

Another quite common method of seat cover fitment is to glue the centre fluted section first before pulling the corners of the cover over as described in the previous paragraphs.

The adhesive used for this centre fixing needs to be of the contact adhesive type. A good trade product for this purpose is one manufactured by Dunlop, having a reference number of S.1358. Each surface to be fixed is spread evenly and thinly with the adhesive; allow it to become 'touch dry' and then bring the two surfaces together, taking care to align the surfaces prior to contact.

The completed cover attached to the seat and ready for use. This Alfa Spider Junior seat has the centre fluted section glued to the foam shape before the border and side panels are pulled into shape and fixed with hog rings

The back of the seat however is fitted in a very unusual manner with the aid of the steel frame. Here the frame is situated inside the wide border of the inside seat back. Metal barbs protrude through the vinyl as it is stretched into position. These are then flattened down as are the three at the top right of the picture.

Once the squab cover including this frame is layed over the seat, the last job is to fit this frame to the seat frame with cup washers and chrome-plated screws

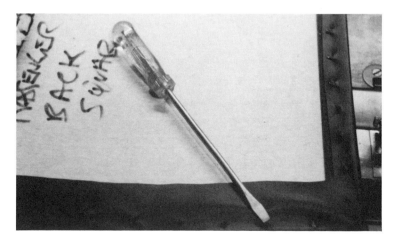

The fixing screws and cup washers for the Alfa Spider seat back. The steel frame mentioned in the previous photographs is located inside the vinyl around the perimeter of the seat

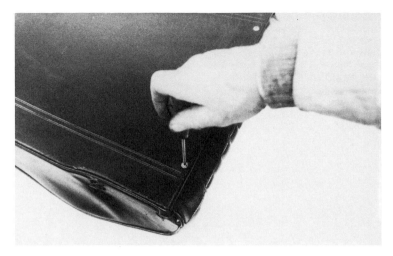

Cover sizing

As with all covers, but in particular those fitted over a Dunlopillo or polyurethane foam upholstery, its size is very important and allowances should be made to make the cover slightly smaller than the actual cushion size.

The amount of allowance will be most determined by the fabric or other material used for the cover, although experience shows where a fabric has a great deal of stretch, that a larger allowance will be necessary. A cover material with much less stretch will require just the reverse.

In the case of the leather cover, as shown in the accompanying photographs an allowance of $\frac{1}{4}$ in. was made, and this then ensured a snug fit over the foam. There is nothing worse than seeing a new seat cover that looks like a rhino's skin, too big and only fitting where it touches.

Clips and fittings employed

Attachment of the seat cover, whether this is one that you have just made or one that you have purchased, is by clips, adhesive or crimped wire hoops better known as hog clips, or a combination of all three.

The clips for attaching fabric to a pressed steel or thin angular frame are shown in the left of the photograph. These are available for various thicknesses of material and seat frame, something just tight enough to hold both together is sufficient, without putting undue strain on the clips. The advantage of clips is that they can easily be

This Bentley S3 driver's seat squab is almost complete regarding fitting. Just a few more clips to be added bottom right and then it remains to trim off the excess leather prior to screwing to the seat cushion for final assembly

Here can be seen seven of the nine hog rings clamping the reinforced edge of the seat cover to the slotted holes in the pressed steel framework. Reinforcement is achieved by the insertion of a plastic rod inside the stitched loop just beneath the hog rings This view shows the wire rings that attach the cover fabric to the rather flimsy pressed steel framework. This framework is held in position just simply by the aid of adhesive

repositioned and the fabric restretched, whereas with adhesive, a great deal more experience is required in order to avoid mistakes.

In the centre of the same photograph is a wire 'hoop' clip. This is to attach fabric to a tubular seat frame. Once fitted, the fabric can be tensioned still further by revolving the hoop clip around the tubular frame.

The use of draw strings

Draw strings are used for the more luxurious appointed

vehicle and are very important where there is need to produce a deep, heavily upholstered effect. Very often this effect is difficult to achieve by any other method and at the same time enable the seat to stand up to the wear and tear of driving.

The draw string is used in conjunction with a reinforcement rod that is situated in a stitched loop on the back of the cover material. Tying off of the draw string needs

To remove the hog rings in order to be able to re-use them, two pairs of long nosed pliers are used/required to carefully prise each ring apart. If they are all going to be replaced, each one can be cut with a pair of side cutters to speed up the stripping down procedure

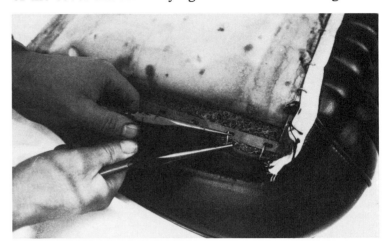

Clips and fittings for seat covers, left and lower centre. Carpet fittings on right. Top centre, door trim board fixing

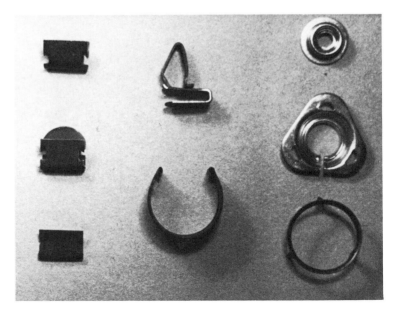

to be accomplished before the back or underside of the seat is covered. Therefore, it is essential that the correct sequence of fitting the cover fabric is followed.

A diagram shows a stitched reinforcement loop of calico (or similar) attached to the seam of the cover material. A

Diagram 13

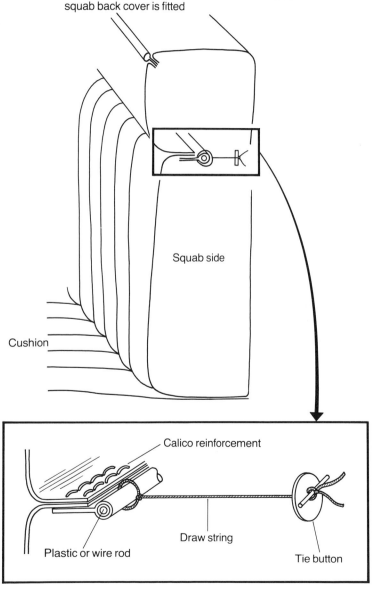

An example where a draw string may be employed. This is fitted, pulled taut and tied off before the seat squab back cover is fitted

Squab side

Cushion

Calico reinforcement

Draw string

Plastic or wire rod

Tie button

This Jensen convertible is an excellent example of the 'natural' look of leather. Finished in cream with matching piping, with the exterior panel work in jet black gloss, a really striking combination.

Where the flutes finish two thirds of the way up the back squab is the sort of position on this type of seat to expect the use of a pair of draw strings.

This enables the deep 'pulled' effect to take place and still stand up to the wear and tear

rod of stout plastic or metal is slid inside this loop and at equidistant points along this rod a loop of strong thread is passed round and tied through the back or underside of the seat. The tension applied to achieve the desired visual effect on the cover and its supporting upholstery is one of personal preference.

Chapter 5 | Soft top hoods

For those with a yen for sports cars, the fabric roof is one area of soft trim that does require specialist skills to manufacture and fit.

The purchase of the more popular car's hood can easily be achieved by mail order from one of the many advertisements published in the classic car enthusiast magazines. This is undoubtedly the method of purchase that initially is very inexpensive.

It is the fitment of each hood that requires almost as much skill as its manufacture and this is where the 'poor' fit often arises. Therefore, it is often worth the additional expense of having your local specialist fit the hood to avoid disappointment. Should there be any problems and you are not completely satisfied with the fitting, at least you do have some redress with the specialist to make amends.

Whether your decision is to fit a hood yourself or pay extra for the specialist, it is the detailed work in hood manufacture that requires careful consideration and indeed investigation before you start.

The most critical factor to look for is the quality of the fabric. This can vary considerably and is often the reason for some of the very attractive offers that may be had.

1   Materials

'Hooding' is the term loosely given to the waterproof material as used for 'soft top' or 'convertible' hoods. Its quality increases as additional layers are added within that piece of fabric thus adding thickness or by the combination of several stronger, more resilient materials.

One such fabric is known as Duck (average quality) and Double Duck (superior quality). The differences between these two hooding fabrics is definitely one of lifespan, coupled with a noticeable difference in heat retention in the cockpit.

A further factor to consider is the frequency a hood is to be moved from its raised position, or its removal altogether. The greater the frequency, the better the quality of hooding you should buy, for if 'Lift-a-dot', press stud, or alternative fittings are often 'activated', the strain put on the surrounding hooding will be significant. Hence, the poorer quality hooding is more likely to give way to splits, tears etc., with heavy use. The majority of soft top hoods prior to approximately 1950 were made of waterproof canvas or a rubberized fabric. Since this period, vinyl covered canvas type material has prevailed in most instances.

The difficulty for restorers is trying to ascertain originality. There aren't many soft top vehicles in the collectable period that haven't at some time or another, had their hoods replaced. When this happened the trimmer often did away with all if not some of the intricate straps and fittings.

How many vehicles for example had their laminated glass rear windows replaced with stitched-in plastic ones?

Search for the signs of removal and replacement of the hood at some stage by inspecting very closely the fittings and fixtures for signs of screws being undone, tacks being replaced and so on. If you really think that your car's soft top is totally original, photograph it and make as many drawings as possible before replacement. It may even pay you to keep the old fabric tucked away in the dry somewhere for future reference, particularly if you are wanting to show the car in concours competition. Proof to judges is sometimes easier with the 'goods' in front of you!

Autojumbles, particularly the big ones, are often good sources of supply for original type fabrics for car hoods, but your nearest trimmer is the first person to approach. He may not have what you want, but can usually put you in touch with a trimmer who specializes in the making of soft top hoods, rather than general interior trimming.

Generally speaking, whatever you are trying to do in the way of restoration, someone else has done before, and it's a matter of trying to locate where these people are. For without exception from my experience, they are only too

Some soft top hood common fittings:

Right On the left the lower self tapping fitment is screwed into the body work, whilst the top two fittings are attached, one on each side of the hooding material. This type of fitment is very effective and puts the minimum amount of strain on the surrounding fabric.

In the centre, the top two fittings are attached, again, one each side of the hooding material and these are then press studded down onto the third fitment which is attached to the bodyshell by way of a 'pop' rivet. This is undoubtedly the most inexpensive hood attachment fitting, but does put a considerable strain on the hood material when removing or refitting the 'convertible' hood. The two fitments lower centre are easy to attach to the hood, for all that is required is the cutting of a small hole with the aid of the appropriate size hollow punch and then screw the back (hidden) to the front section. The lower screw fitting is for the bodywork. On the right there are the three components that make up the turn button system of hood attachment. The lower fitment is screwed or pop riveted to the bodyshell whilst the top two fittings are fixed, again one either side of the hood fabric. The turn button requires little effort to use and fitting is relatively easy. However, they are not the most attractive fittings and are a nuisance when it comes to cleaning the car. Having said this, the criterion should always be the fitment of as near as possible to the original particularly if one is contemplating entering competition. Incidentally, the fittings shown are normal size

Below This close up of some of the hood fittings shows the good standard of plating applied by the manufacturers to assist with the fittings needs to stand up to the elements. Most are nickle-plated, but some are chromium-plated. Inspect each fitting to ensure that the plating process has been carried out successfully, otherwise the rust will follow quickly behind!

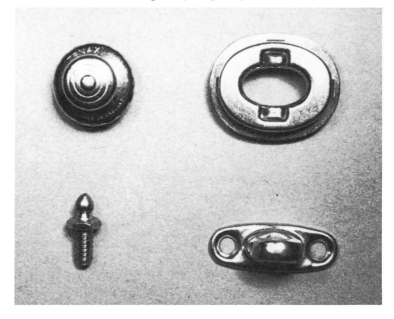

willing to come forward with information, advice and general assistance to help you with your problems. It's amazing how a chat with somebody who's had that experience or similar problem can alleviate your problem.

So bear all these factors in mind to enable the most satisfying choice to be made.

As for the fittings on the hood, the 'Lift-a-dot' probably causes the least wear on the surrounding hood fabric. However, these are more expensive and are thus more likely to be fitted to the superior hood.

One last thing to look for when looking for quality, is the extent of reinforcement with additional fabric and/or stitching. This should be prominent where any possible abrasion is apparent, i.e., wherever the hood comes into contact with the frame, fixings etc. The easiest way to look for a comparison is to see where the old hood of your car

The TR4 with hood fully removed

Framework for the TR hood is situated behind and around the rear seat, giving the uncluttered and unobtrusive look

has failed and see if the new hood is sufficiently reinforced at those points of excessive wear.

Some hoods have a 'bound' edge, similar in appearance to the bound edge on carpets. This does two things, firstly it gives considerable additional strength to the edge of the hood fabric, often the weakest part, and secondly is very pleasing to look at, as it carefully tidies the hood's appearance.

2 Stowable hoods

The accompanying photographs are those taken of a unique Triumph TR4 belonging to Geoff Palmer. One of the features that makes this car unique (apart from the way in which it has carefully been restored), is the method of hood fitment. This is one of a few soft top hood fitments that is taken off completely from the hood frame when

A small hook is employed,
situated just in front of the
thumb, to ensure that the side of
the hood does not flap or leak

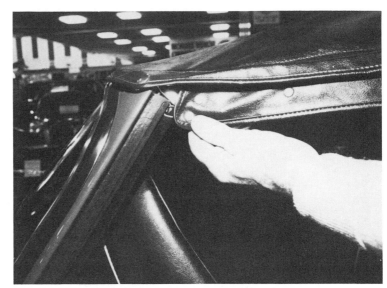

The rear seat squab is then
raised, the cushion hinged
forward, to reveal the hood
frame and straps

A pair of 'tension' straps should be positioned next, one each side of the car, but only at the rear of the hood

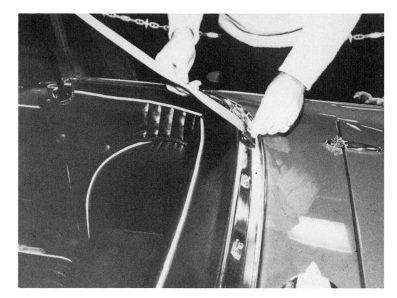

Geoff is seen here raising the hood hoops into their respective positions

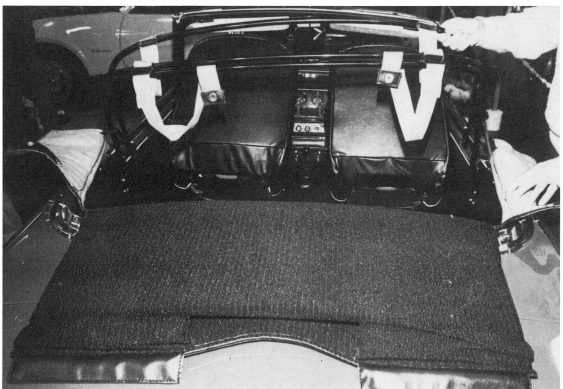

With frame almost in the erected position, the hood is carefully laid in position over the hood hoops or sticks

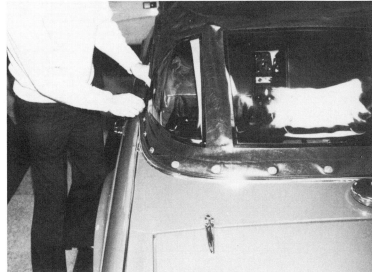

Having hooked the fixing bar, attached to the front of the hood, to the top of the windscreen frame, the skirt of the hood is progressively attached to the Lift-a-dot fittings on the body scuttle

This internal shot of the underside of the hood depicts the press stud fitting ready to be attached to the front hood stick. This fitment is actually stitched to the front hood panel seam. The purpose of this fitment is to reduce, if not eliminate the risk of the hood billowing up and lifting at speed

Sunbeam Tiger with a fabric hood. Most of this fits quite well, but the limited use of just two Lift-a-dot fittings situated around the hood skirt are not sufficient to hold this area down without 'lifting' occurring. Also the rear screen is not taut enough in the horizontal plane leaving many creases.

Not only are these faults unpleasant to view, they are often the first signs of leaks on the hood skirt, whilst the creased windows make it difficult to see through and not easy to keep clean

lowered and stored in a separate bag housed in the boot of the car.

It is because of the 'removal' from the car that the hood is kept in such good condition. There is no severe creasing or squashing by the hoop frames as with the 'in situ' type fitments. It does have a small disadvantage in that the hood may take longer to erect, particularly when trying to beat a sudden downpour.

Two views of one of the best tailored soft top hoods of this type to be seen

**Poor fitting. What to avoid.
An example of a new hood as
fitted to a Triumph Spitfire, but
compare how the N/S quarter
light window sits nice and taut
whereas the O/S is slack in one
direction and very tight in the
vertical direction causing
unsightly creases**

Nonetheless, this type of hood fitment does have a number of 'worthwhile' features, such as the clean and uncluttered lines of the hood, both in the erected and removed positions, the latter often an eyesore of unwanted fabric and mechanism. The 'Lift-a-dot' fittings around the base of the hood ensure less effort is exerted on the hood fabric, ensuring a longer life expectancy. Then there are the small and often unnoticed features, as highlighted in the photographs, of the very small fittings attaching the front hoop by means of press studs. Both of these features help to ensure that the vehicle will be leak free, draught free and relatively 'flap' or noise free. Very often none of these features will be found on cheaper quality hoods. So look out for these when deciding what to purchase.

3 Repairs

If the cost of a new hood is prohibitive or uneconomical for you, then the problems of splits or tears caused by sharp protrusions, vandalism etc., can be overcome with a relatively small outlay with a 'reinforced repair'. However, it must be stressed that the remainder of the hood fabric must be in good, sound condition in order to accomplish a strong repair.

This type of repair can be carried out by your local trimmer, although should you wish to tackle the job yourself this is the method to adopt.

Remove the hood from the vehicle and turn it upside down on to a clean and unobstructed work bench.

To affect the reinforced repair, stretch out the damaged

Diagram 14   **Soft Top Hoods – Reinforced repairs**

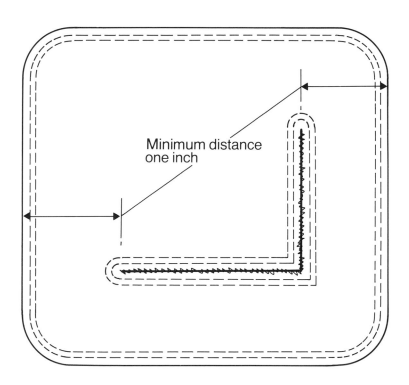

Minimum distance one inch

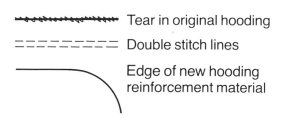

Tear in original hooding

Double stitch lines

Edge of new hooding reinforcement material

area and assess the size of reinforcement required. This needs to be larger than the split or tear by at least one inch all round and can be made from suitable hooding material. Make sure that the corners of the new material to be attached are radiussed to reduce the risk of the corners lifting under tension.

Having marked out and cut to shape the reinforcement patch, turn the hood over to reveal the face or top side. Place a length of adhesive tape over the join, but only as a temporary measure!

Reverse the hood to the wrong side again and apply adhesive to both the damaged area and the reinforcement patch. When touch dry, press the two surfaces firmly

With the hood in the down position on this early Ford Model A American roadster everything lays in line like a good battalion of soldiers. You can look both inside and outside this hood and it is as near perfection as possible

The hood of this Talbot 90 has seen many years of use and is still very serviceable. The only reason to change at this stage is to brighten up the colour as it has faded rather badly

together, finishing off by hitting downwards with the face of a small hammer to ensure good adhesion.

Remove the temporary tape from the face side. This will have achieved two things. Firstly, this will have prevented the adhesive from leaking out on to the exterior hood surface and, secondly, the tape will have assisted in holding the repaired area together whilst being glued.

Once this stage has been completed, it remains to place a double row of stitches around the reinforcement patch and the split or tear. Make sure that the thread used is the same colour as the hood and then the repair will hardly be noticeable.

Refit the hood for the final stage of the repair. In order to ensure that the holes made by the stitching are leakproof, it is necessary to spray these with a silicon spray, or rub in some dubbin or suitable alternative. Therefore, with the hood back in its correct position, taut and with the new reinforced repair complete with waterproofing agent, a long and serviceable life should be expected.

Chapter 6 | Carpets—Choosing, cutting, binding

Assuming that you have access to an industrial sewing machine, carpet renovation is easy to have a go at, almost always with very rewarding results for remarkably little effort.

1 Carpet selection

The floor covering of any vehicle will normally be governed by three factors: vehicle type, vehicle usage, vehicle purchase cost.

A utility vehicle will usually be furbished with the cheapest covering possible, usually moulded rubber floor coverings.

Likewise, a vehicle designed to a higher specification, and yet required to be an 'all round' vehicle, will often be fitted with carpets having rubber 'inserts' or overstitched rubber sections for durability.

Limousines and high quality 'up market' vehicles will undoubtedly be floored with Wilton or similar top quality carpet.

A point to remember is that the carpets generally fitted to the mass production car were of the rubber backed, one piece nature, which doesn't fray. More expensive carpet with its separate underlay is much more likely to fray. Hence the need to bind this type of carpet, although this can double up as a decorative feature, too.

The binding of carpets is only really possible where the stitch length can be in the region of 5 or 6 to the inch; this means that the pile of the carpet has to be of good quality and density. The density has to be sufficient to 'hide' the stitching, and this can only be achieved with success on high quality carpet. Top quality is expensive.

Sumptuous Wilton carpet fitted to a Bentley four-door saloon. Binding of the edges of the carpet can be seen on both the front and rear pieces

Because of the high price, per metre, of quality carpet it is virtually impossible to compete with companies producing carpet kits, although these kits are generally only available for the more popular car. Just be selective in choosing if you decide to buy 'ready-mades'. Often good value but many rarely fit! As with many other purchases of this type, it is often best if you can see someone else's vehicle that has been fitted with a particular company's ready-mades. Use your judgement.

2 Removal

Prior to commencing the renewal of carpets for your vehicle, it will be necessary to remove both front and rear seats (if fitted). Depending on the age of the car, this can be an extremely difficult job, particularly when seat runners are bolted through to the floor direct. These fixings may be by bolts threaded into cage or welded nuts to the floor pan, or may just be straight nuts and bolts. Whichever the case, they will often be found to be in poor state due to the weathering that the car has had over the years.

Similarly, seat belt mountings on later vehicles present the same 'seized-up' problems. Therefore apply a freeing agent to the threads protruding through under the floor and do this a few days before your plan to remove the carpets. This is something that cannot be rushed if you want to cause the minimum amount of damage.

Having left the penetrating/freezing fluid for two or three days, wire brush the protruding thread, which should remove the excess oxide and corrosion. Undo the bolts from the inside of the car. You may need the assistance of a friend if separate nuts and bolts have been fitted.

If, as is possibly the case, the bolts will still not shift, then alternative methods should be attempted. If you have access to oxy-acetylene welding equipment or a good quality butane torch or similar, then use this to heat up the nut to a cherry red colour on the underside of the car. Take great care not to use the heat-source near fuel lines, brake pipes, cables etc. Using this method rarely fails, as the action of the heat expands the nut which on cooling contracts again. This expansion and contraction is normally sufficient to start the removal of the nut or bolt.

Should you not have any of the foregoing equipment, then one or a number of the following methods have to be attempted.

Shock treatment

With the assistance of someone holding a counter weight against the nut on the underside of car, give the head of the bolt a few sharp hits with a hammer and drift, then try to remove the bolt.

Stripping out the seats and seat belt anchorage points of this two-door Mercedes warrants the care already mentioned, but especially when the vehicle is becoming rare, out of production and expensive!

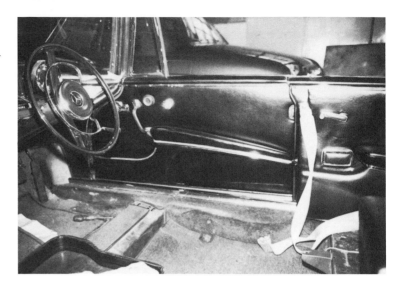

Removal by drilling
Centre punch the centre of bolt, proceed to drill out, commencing with a small 'pilot' drill, increasing the size to the thread size of the bolt.

Seat belt dangers
If you contemplate heating up a seat belt anchorage bolt, great care must be taken not to melt any nylon washers that may be present and likewise the seat belt webbing itself is liable to melt if excess heat is applied!

Having removed the front seats and/or seat belts, (this being one of the most difficult parts of carpet replacement) lift out rear seat if fitted and carefully lift out the old carpet pieces. No matter what condition the old carpets are in, try and keep them as intact as possible if you want to use them as patterns.

Typical layouts and joint areas
The width of the car will govern the most economical use of the new carpet. A sports car for example will usually employ two side strips of carpet, with a further three strips, one for the propshaft tunnel, and one each for each inner door sill. Two additional pieces may also be used, one along the heel board and the other over the gearbox.

Saloon cars, on the other hand, usually have a front section the full width of the car, and a rear section, also the full width.

Carpets fitted to vehicles in the mid to late 1960s to early 1970s, were often of the moulded type. These are produced by putting sheets of carpet in a hot press, the shape being the same profile as the floor pan of the car it is being produced for. The only way to replace these is with a new moulded carpet set, purchased from your local supplier, possibly your franchised dealer or from one of the specialists in the manufacture of pattern carpets.

When measuring up for the carpet, remember to take into account (if fitted) the lower edges of the doors and the vertical section of the heel board. This is the panel that is situated beneath the rear seat and acts as the support for the front of the seat.

3 Cutting lines—allowances for door bottoms, etc.

Carpets, as with all other trim fabrics, are supplied in standard widths and it is with this in mind that cutting lines should be considered.

Most car carpets are supplied in either 48 or 54 in. widths and as such one wants to make the best use to avoid wastage, but consideration also has to be given to the 'knap' of the carpet to ensure that the 'flow' of colour looks the same, wherever it is viewed from.

The diagram shows the carpet as layed out for a 1960 Mini. (The difference between the carpets for an early Mini compared to one that was built some years later is that an additional two holes are required. One is for the starter solenoid button situated on the floor, and the other, a hole for the foot operated dipswitch. Both of these components eventually moved on to the dashboard and finally the steering column.) The arrows show the direction of the knap to ensure colour continuity.

When it is necessary to cover the floor of a wide vehicle, very often the maximum width of carpet is insufficient to cover the distance. Consequently the carpet is turned through 90 degrees and the knap runs from side to side with the join underneath the front seats.

It is the larger more luxurious vehicles that are more likely to have the lower section of the door trim covered

Diagram 15   **Carpet Layout – 1960 Mini**

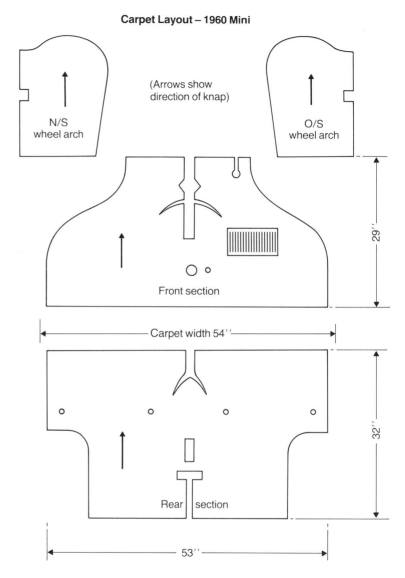

(Arrows show
direction of knap)

N/S
wheel arch

O/S
wheel arch

29″

Front section

Carpet width 54″

32″

Rear   section

53″

with the same carpet as fitted to the floor of the vehicle.

In this accompanying diagram, the carpet width, knap and allowances for the door bottoms are all clearly marked. Make sure, particularly as the patterns have to be marked out on the underside of the carpet, that the knap runs in the same direction for both the front and rear carpet as mistakes are easily made. Always double check after mark-

Diagram 16

Carpet Layout – 1954 Bentley

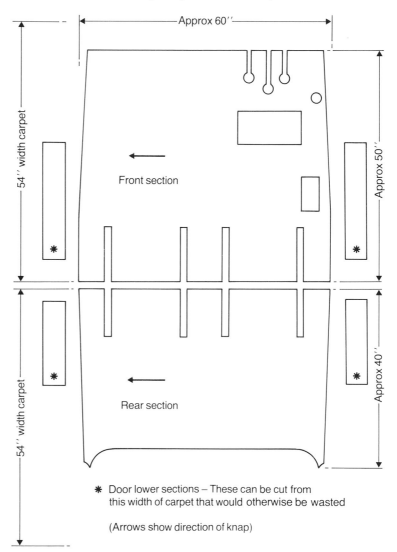

Approx 60''

54'' width carpet

Approx 50''

Front section

54'' width carpet

Approx 40''

Rear section

✳ Door lower sections – These can be cut from this width of carpet that would otherwise be wasted

(Arrows show direction of knap)

ing out prior to cutting.

Use of knives

Having marked out on the underside of the new carpet and checked for fit and knap, it is now time to cut the carpet to shape. This can be achieved with scissors, but to be able to complete a really clean cut, only a knife can assist with this.

For the 'one off' job, a Stanley-type knife with disposable blade is quite adequate, but if much of this work is contemplated a trimmer's knife that can be re-sharpened on an oilstone will be found to be more adaptable and versatile. Whichever knife is used, always ensure that the other hand supporting the carpet and carpet and straight edge, is beside or behind the cutting action of the knife.

Cutting the carpet needs to be carried out on a firm cutting surface, i.e. a wooden bench. This, together with the sharp knife, gives quick accurate results with a one stroke cut through the carpet.

Templates—use of old carpets

Should your vehicle be decidedly unhealthy and the carpets long since gone, then templates made from stout paper (a spare roll of wallpaper is very useful for this task) will be necessary.

The most awkward area for the template will be around and above the pedals and steering column position. Great care must be taken to ensure that where the pedal travel is through the floor, that freedom of movement is not restricted, otherwise the car may become unsafe.

Another point to consider when dealing with vehicles of the 1940s and the early 1950s is that of draughts. Much of the draught in these vehicles was up and around the bulkhead area of the car. It pays to have a thorough look under the dashboard at the bulkhead area to see if the carpet can be taken that little bit higher to cover up the various holes that there will be present.

Now you have reached the stage of having removed all the seats and seat belts, remove the old carpet and have this ready for a pattern or alternatively have paper templates made, it is time to decide whether you are going to purchase a set of carpets from the growing number of people supplying ready-mades, or whether you are going to buy carpet and trim this yourself.

Whichever you decide, authenticity in appearance should be paramount. Some vehicles such as the Morris Minor have virtually no bound edges, whereas the vehicles that were manufactured to a higher specification such as the contemporary Riley, or Wolseley had almost all edges of the carpet bound. As a general rule, rubber backed car-

Practice on a scrap piece of carpet when you wish to carry out binding. Even when one is familiar with binding, this is still necessary to obtain the correct thread tension. The actual carpet shown here is a good quality grey carpet fitted to Jaguars. Burgundy binding was used for the dark area and grey for the light area

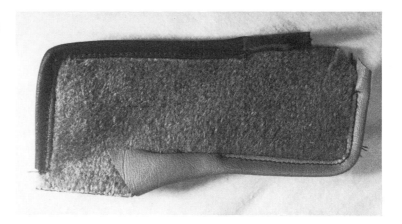

pets do not need binding whereas woven carpets are subject to fraying if binding is not carried out.

Assuming that you have made the decision to cut and bind your own carpets and have chosen the type and colour, lay the carpet face down. Lay templates or old carpet patterns *upside down*. Mark carefully. Check! Make sure that all is correct and patterns are laid accurately.

Cut the relevant pieces with a good sharp pair of scissors or knife.

4   Binding

The edge of the carpet can be bound to compliment the colour of the carpet or an alternative contrasting colour can be adopted. For example, grey carpet, with a black binding. But remember to identify what the available colours were at the time of vehicle manufacture.

There are three methods of binding and each is designed for use in different situations:

1 For the more prestigious car there are no visible stitches in the upper or face side of the binding.
2 One row of stitches showing in the binding. Because of the edge of the carpet, rounding difficult corners is made easier.
3 This only has one row of stitches in total which are visible. Best suited for use on lightweight or very thin carpets but not very easy for those of you who are all fingers and thumbs.

Joins in binding

Leather binding requires a special technique for joining unlike any other material.

With the material face down and with the aid of a very sharp knife or razor blade, pare off the back with a tapering action. The other piece to be joined is pared off on the face side, again tapering off. The two pieces are then laid end to end as and when the joint needs to be made on the edge of the carpet. When binding is complete, this type of join should be unnoticeable.

Joins in other fabrics are carried out in a similar manner to those used in piping, i.e., the two pieces to be joined are stitched together prior to machining onto the carpet. (Refer to the diagram.)

Points to remember when binding:

1 No raw edges to be visible (this applies to all trimming).
2 The minimum distance of the binding visible on the face side of the carpet should not be less than $\frac{5}{16}$ in. This ensures that movement of the workpiece through the machine is controllable and that there is no risk of the stitching pulling off the edge of the carpet.
3 Don't pull the binding too tight when machining, as this will make the carpet turn up at the corners, not allowing it to lay flat.

Diagram 17   Binding Carpets – Alternative methods

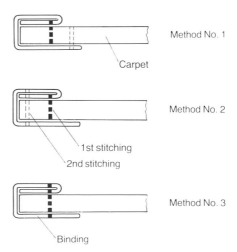

Method No. 1

Carpet

Method No. 2

1st stitching

2nd stitching

Method No. 3

Binding

4 Keep the speed of the machine steady and controllable and if necessary, wind the machine over by hand on difficult sections, especially tight corners and curves.

5 Make joins unobtrusive, i.e. underneath seats, or make sure if they are visible that they are positioned sensibly, perhaps centrally on one side.

6 If very heavy, good quality carpet is anticipated, it may be necessary to oil the thread. Most industrial machines have a reservoir on top of the machine which the thread passes through prior to making its way down to the needle. This ensures that the thread is lubricated as it passes through the binding and carpet thus ensuring that the thread does not drag and break.

Diagram 18

Method of joining Carpet Binding/Piping Strips

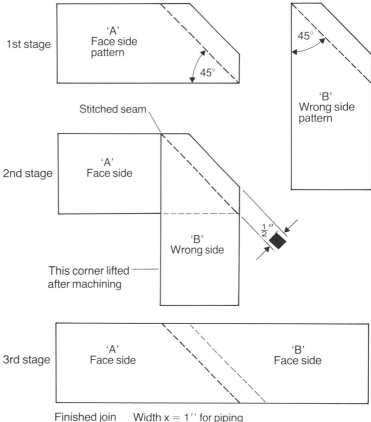

The bound edge of the carpets in this 1940 Chevy shows just how crisp and clean fitting they should be, even down to the binding round the hole of the brake pedal!

5 Fitting carpets

The main areas of carpet, that is on the floor area itself, can be fitted and fixed in a number of ways. The most common methods being by carpet clip fittings, one on each corner, or self tapping screws with cup washers. The inner sills, prop-shaft tunnel and front wheelarches are usually attached with an adhesive, a 'contact' adhesive applied to both the back of the carpet and the area to be attached. This should be left until touch dry.

The application of the adhesive should be done with plenty of fresh air circulating to ensure that one is not overcome with fumes.

Care should be taken to align the carpet prior to being positioned, as it is difficult to reposition once attached! Any excess of adhesive on areas of the car that are visible can be removed with the aid of a clean lint-free cloth and petrol.

6   Replace or restore

To replace or restore is often a difficult decision, but the carpets shown in this Pontiac GTO at first sight look a right mess.

With further investigation it was found to have little signs of wear and tear and the biggest problem was one of dampness causing a fungus to grow. The water leak that caused this problem will also leave some heavy staining and will therefore require some treatment.

Firstly, get rid of the water leak! Secondly, remove the carpet from the vehicle (taking note of the necessary steps required), give the carpet a thorough shampoo, rinse and leave to dry in a well-ventilated and warm atmosphere.

If you are lucky enough to be able to borrow a vacuum cleaner that is capable of sucking up liquids, then draw as much moisture out as possible prior to drying. If this is not possible, wait until the carpet is dry and then with the aid of a stiff brush, vacuum clean well.

This will probably leave you with a clean carpet, but with a number of water marks or stains. The latter can then be stained with the appropriate dye, in the case of the Pontiac this would be black. The dye can be daubed on with a small foam sponge until sufficient colour has bled into the carpet fibres in order to obliterate the stain.

Note that the use of dye stuffs should be tried out on an area of the carpet that is unseen, say under the front seats, to ensure the possibility of a good match!

Rubber floor coverings

Most utility vehicles together with a number of the economy versions of non-utility vehicles produced since 1945, had rubber or rubber type floor covering in order to accommodate rough wear and tear in all sorts of weather conditions.

Delivery vehicles are a classic example where the driver is constantly in and out of the vehicle. This results in water, mud etc. being walked and ground into the floor covering.

When rubber floor coverings are frequently washed and kept relatively free of dirt, few problems arise. Rather it is when dirt and mud are left to collect and build that rapid wear takes place.

Due to a bad water leak, the carpets of this Pontiac GTO have grown a considerable fungus. However, apart from this the carpet is in remarkably good condition and therefore an attempt should be made to wash, dry, hoover and stain as described in the text

A closer view of the Pontiac carpet shows how much of a hold the fungus has

To refurbish existing rubber mats, a modern paint suitable for covering plastic and rubber is acceptable, but preferably sprayed on with a spray gun to give an even distribution.

Should there be only a slight deterioration then shoe polish of the correct colour makes a grand job.

The biggest problem with rubber mats is the wear that occurs around the driver's heels. This usually results in holes through the rubber. If these are not too large, the ever useful cycle, motorcycle, car or even commercial vehicle cold, vulcanized patch on the underside gives remarkable results.

To build up the wear on the top side of the rubber use a smaller feather edge patch and then apply plenty of solution around the perimeter of this in order to build up the thickness. Finally, spray the surface as mentioned earlier with paint suitable for covering plastic and rubber.

If all else fails and the rubber mats for your vehicle are either missing or in such a poor state as to be irreparable, then replacements can be purchased. Should your vehicle be obscure, then approaching a manufacturer of rubber mats with a view to supplying a number of people in your club may be the answer to your problem.

Obviously, to make the mould for just one product would be too costly, so seek the needs of clubs, friends, etc, to obtain sufficient numbers to make the cost of manufacture viable.

Index